# THE BUSY MUM'S COOKBOOK

# THE BUSY MUM'S COOKBOOK

### Easy, quick and delicious recipes for families with hectic lives

## Mary Gwynn

SIMON &
SCHUSTER
ILLUSTRATED

London · New York · Sydney · Toronto

A CBS COMPANY

First published in Great Britain by Simon & Schuster
UK Ltd, 2011
A CBS COMPANY

1 3 5 7 9 10 8 6 4 2

SIMON & SCHUSTER
ILLUSTRATED BOOKS
Simon & Schuster UK Ltd
222 Gray's Inn Road
London
WC1X 8HB

www.simonandschuster.co.uk

Simon & Schuster Australia
Sydney

Editorial director: Francine Lawrence
Project editor: Sharon Amos
Designer: Meg Georgeson
Photography: David Merewether
Stylist: Cherry Whytock
Production manager: Katherine Thornton
Commercial director: Ami Richards

A CIP catalogue record for this book is available
from the British Library

ISBN 978-0-85720-353-3

Printed and bound in China
Colour reproduction by Dot Gradations Ltd, UK

## thank you

I've had a huge amount of support writing this very personal book so I must thank my family, friends and the team who helped me all the way.

I am so grateful to the recipe testers and tasters who ensured the recipes do what they say: my two daughters, Lucy and Isobel; my sister Lucy; and Cherry Wellesley.

Huge thanks to our photography team: the wonderful David Merewether, who took the stunning photos, and stylist Cherry Whytock for finding plates and pots to complement my own dishes, many courtesy of Mica Macey and Le Petit Jardin, Tunbridge Wells. And to all the friends and neighbours roped in as background models.

Thanks, too, to the supportive team at Simon & Schuster Illustrated; to the calm and brilliant copy editor Sharon Amos; and to art director Meg Georgeson for designing such beautiful pages. To my friend and agent, Heather Holden-Brown for holding my hand and listening at moments of stress; and to Alison Oakervee, food editor at Waitrose, for commissioning the recipe cards that give me the impetus to write this book.

Finally, my family – all of whom have played a vital part. I wouldn't have been a busy mum without them, but I want to thank them for understanding the strains of writing, testing and photographing such a cookery book from our home. In particular, Lucy, for being such a capable assistant food stylist for the photography, as well as modelling when required. And my husband Derek, for creating the original visuals that brought the book to life, for putting up with the kitchen being turned into a photography studio for a month, and for his sound advice – and for all his enduring love and support.

# contents

# busy mum's
# basics

A year or two ago, a working friend with two small children begged me to make her a shopping list of the basic ingredients I keep in my kitchen cupboard, and provide her with a set of simple inexpensive recipes that she could cook easily and quickly after a busy day's teaching and, most important, that her offspring would eat. Around the same time my sister (no mean cook herself) asked me how I always managed to create something wonderful for lunch every day with what I magicked out of the fridge. Their questions started me thinking: what are the tips that have worked for me for nearly quarter of a century as a busy mum?

Since first joining the ranks of the guilt laden – otherwise known as working mothers – I've had countless incarnations in the role, and have recently returned to where I started out, as a full-time food writer. With daughters now 23 and 21 and a stepson of 16, I am still discovering new challenges – and joys – to the whole business. I've worked full time, part time, run my own business from home, and advised various companies across the country as a consultant. I've been part of a stress-ridden two-parent family, an even more stress-ridden single mother, and an occasionally irate stepmother (yoga works, believe me). There've been moments of total despair, but also many times of joy and exhilaration, and we have managed to laugh a lot – often it seemed while crying at the same time. And I now have three wonderfully balanced, successful and charming young adults, who all eat everything set in front of them, know how to behave when they are invited out and – what is more – are enjoying cooking for themselves. So I must have done something right!

Yet until recently, I worried that I had reared two daughters (and a part-time son) who loved to eat but seemed to have no desire to cook. I needn't have fretted. Once they had to fend for themselves, I realised I had bestowed on them the best gift of all – one that Sleeping Beauty's fairy godmothers seem to have missed. All three have grown into adventurous gourmets who search out interesting dishes and are happy to try unusual ingredients. They enjoy food in a social setting, as something to be savoured with family and friends. Each had her or his fussy moments, turned up noses, refused dishes that I'd slaved over, seemed to exist on either air or junk for periods of time, but this has passed into the mists. With a bit more time to reflect, I realised a simple and vital truth: cooking your own food gives you freedom to choose how, what and when you feed your family. And by teaching children to eat properly and enjoy good food, you are setting them up for life. They will have to learn how to cook for themselves to maintain the standards you have given them! Now that's good parenting…

My sister's and my friend's requests prompted me to start thinking about the endless planning, shopping and cooking I'd done over the years. And so this is *The Busy Mum's Cookbook* – a distillation of my own years of experience as cook, mum, food writer and, just as important, daughter of parents who themselves enjoy good food.

The recipes in these pages are all based around a simple store cupboard of everyday ingredients. Each chapter has a theme reflecting the different demands for all types of meals. Some days you will be shopping and cooking at the end of a working day, maybe with food bought in a rush on the way home; at other times a meal needs to be created from what

Their questions started me thinking about the endless planning, shopping and cooking I'd done over the years

you have to hand or you may be feeding smaller children before preparing a meal for you and your partner. Flexibility is essential! Anyone who has teenagers knows the challenge of suddenly being faced with six or so 'starving' extras half an hour before you were planning a night in front of the telly with a boiled egg on a tray.

All mums work by definition – and that's before you even begin to consider taking on paid employment. Full time, part time, volunteer, carer – what many of us lack is time and, increasingly, skill and confidence in the kitchen. But we share a common goal: the desire to feed our families food that is good for them and, even more important, that they will eat. We want meals that are quick to plan, shop for and prepare – and fit a budget that is getting tighter. Above all, they must taste really good too. Families should always enjoy what they sit down to eat – hopefully together.

With this in mind, I've tried to ensure that the majority of these recipes contain no more than eight ingredients (apart from seasoning, oil, butter, etc) with three or four short steps to the method. On the whole, they can be prepared and cooked in 30 minutes or less (or else come with very quick prep time and then a longer cooking time that doesn't need supervision, so you can be bathing children, reading a bedtime story or supervising homework). I've aimed to fit within current healthy-eating guidelines (with a few exceptions for occasional treats) and keep to a reasonable budget. The recipes serve one, two, four or six, but are designed to be easy to convert to serve more if needed.

The recipes come from years of research and experimentation. Contributions appear from most members of my family; others come from friends and colleagues, often handed over on scruffy food-stained notes or passed on by word of mouth. I've gleaned ideas from favourite, now out-of-print, cookbooks and adapted them to suit my own circumstances and taste.

The majority I've created myself to answer a particular need or occasion. They come tried and tested by me, often under pressure, so you can learn from my own experience. I've included plenty of tips on when to take short cuts (I don't like the word 'cheat' – it feels dishonest), when to freeze dishes for later and advice on how to adapt the recipes for different tastes: though I do draw the line at preparing different meals for various family members – that way lies disaster.

With a little planning you can turn your store cupboard into a magical Aladdin's cave, ready for you to delve into and keep the whole family well fed, healthy and happy.

# Store cupboard essentials

## Soy sauce
Look for a brewed soy sauce rather than a chemically produced version, for intense flavour. Like most ingredients, the higher the price, the better the quality, so you can adopt the less is more approach. You save in the end, as the sauce will go further.

## Potatoes/sweet potatoes
The secret with potatoes is choosing the right one for the job in hand. Old and floury or young and waxy – the former for light but crispy roast potatoes and creamy mashes (rather than gluey pastes) and the latter when you need a bit of texture such as in a tortilla, in salads or the sausage casserole on page 141. Store them out of their bags in a dark place so they don't sweat, and discard any green ones.

Use sweet potatoes in the same way – roasted, mashed, in soups or tossed into salads. They can be just scrubbed and baked in their skins for a really healthy veg or replace regular potatoes in dishes such as the hash on page 64.

## Onions
Red, brown, white, shallots, salad – I usually keep a selection of each. The flesh of red onions is sweeter when eaten raw and they add colour to cooked dishes. Use shallots for an intense onion flavour in a delicate sauce or stuffing or try them roasted.

## Pasta
What did our grandmothers do without pasta? When I was a child the only pasta I ate regularly came in a can with tomato sauce. Now we are completely overwhelmed with choice. To keep it simple I suggest you buy a small selection of really good Italian dried pasta made with durum wheat. It will be noticeably better both in flavour and texture than a cheaper variety when cooked. Spaghetti or linguine, macaroni, lasagne and a short shape such as penne will do. There seems to be some rules about which shape to serve with what, but don't worry too

much about that. Just think about how the eater will manage and how much might end up on the table or floor. Follow pack instructions for cooking but do use as large a pan of boiling water as possible and keep it boiling merrily or the pasta will stick.

## Canned Italian tomatoes

I was lucky enough to visit Naples on a trip to write about the local tomato harvest. This area of Italy is ideal for growing varieties for canning. The process captures the wonderful intense flavour of perfectly ripe tomatoes – much better for cooking than bland fresh tomatoes grown out of season. The canning process also releases lycopene, a valuable antioxidant, making canned tomatoes a better source of lycopene than raw. Canned tomatoes are an easy way to give the family one of their five-a-day fruit and veg. Choose Italian-grown chopped tomatoes for quick sauces and pizza toppings, and the whole plum ones for longer-cooked dishes when the flavour can develop.

## Butternut squash

Definitely in my top five ingredients, butternut squash is a relative newcomer to our tables and, boy, have I embraced it! I love its sweet dense flesh – so comforting in soups and risottos. It's a perfect store cupboard ingredient and will keep for four to six weeks in a cool dark cupboard (not the fridge).

With their bulbous shape they can be tricky to peel, so avoid really large ones. Cut them in half from stalk to base with a heavy knife, then peel and remove the seeds. You can buy ready peeled and cubed squash for an emergency but remember that any veg starts to lose its vitamins and goodness once cut – so for preference buy frozen ready-prepared.

## Rice

Basmati, risotto and Thai sticky rice all have a place in my store cupboard. For best results it is really worth using the right rice for the dish you are making. Risottos, pilaffs and paella recipes naturally evolved from the ingredients to hand in their country of origin so why go against the grain? (Excuse the pun!) Again,

buy the best you can afford and cook them properly. Read the pack instructions: good food companies have spent a lot of time working out the best way to cook their product.

## Chickpeas

Buy canned chickpeas for convenience. Choose those canned in water without salt. I always have a pack of dried chickpeas in my cupboard, and every couple of years when I check through the shelves, there they are, out of date. You do get better texture soaking them and cooking from scratch, and it is cheaper – but life is somehow too short.

## Herbs and spices

Fresh herbs make a huge difference to lots of dishes, but buying them in small packs at the supermarket can be expensive and, more often than not, they sit in the salad drawer, only to be thrown out when they've deteriorated.

If you can, try to grow your own – either in the garden or in pots on the windowsill. My essentials are flat-leaf parsley (much better flavour and easier to chop than traditional curly), mint, chives, sage, thyme and rosemary. The best alternatives to fresh are the newly available bags of frozen chopped herbs now in supermarkets, rather than jars of dried. I keep chives, mint and amazingly useful ready-chopped root ginger in my freezer.

Unless you cook curries on a regular basis (more than once a week), a good curry powder or paste will be fine. Then keep cumin, crushed chillies, coriander, cinnamon and ground ginger to hand, too.

## Olive oil

Oils lose their flavour after a while and, in the case of nut oils and really good extra-virgin olive oil, can go rancid. Buy large bottles of a reasonable-quality olive oil for general use, and keep a small bottle of a really good extra-virgin oil for adding seasoning and flavour to soups, salads and pasta dishes. You also need a bottle of something relatively tasteless such as groundnut oil, for stir-frying and curries. Store oils in a cool dark place to keep them at their best.

### Lentils

Lentils are the perfect staple: no need to soak, quick to cook, a valuable source of protein, vitamins, etc and – wonderful for the cook – the different varieties can be served in so many ways. Use them in soups, salads and stews, or to partner grilled meats.

### Nuts

Pecans, walnuts and ground almonds add texture, protein and flavour to countless dishes. Ideal as a source of useful protein for non-meat eaters, nuts have a high oil content, which means that they do go off. So keep them in a cool dark place, in well-sealed packs. Buy small amounts so you don't end up throwing them away. Pine nuts (kernels rather than true nuts) add bite to salads. Toast them to bring out their flavour: I dry fry them in a small pan – if I try to do it in the oven I always end up burning them.

### Lemons

Lemon zest and fresh lemon juice are an essential part of a cook's palette of flavours. To understand what I mean try the cake on page 198 and compare it to a bought version. Or toss freshly cooked pasta with good olive oil, a little chilli and garlic and the grated rind and juice of a lemon. That's real fast food!

## Fridge essentials

### Minced beef

Over the years as a food writer I've had to write the classic '50 ways with mince' types of recipes and yet I still go back to the holy trinity of Bolognese (either with spaghetti or made into lasagne), chilli and cottage pie. I've included my versions here: I couldn't have written this book without them and I think they stand up as models of their kind!

Always buy a good-quality steak mince with a bit of fat. Cheap mince is nasty and greasy with no flavour, so the cost saving is nullified by the unpleasant result – while minced lean steak is too

## The working mum's top 25 essential ingredients

**Store cupboard essentials**

* Soy sauce
* Potatoes/sweet potatoes
* Onions
* Pasta
* Canned Italian tomatoes
* Butternut squash
* Rice
* Chickpeas
* Herbs and spices
* Olive oil
* Lentils
* Nuts – ground almonds/peanuts/ cashews/walnuts/pecans
* Lemons

**Fridge essentials**

* Minced beef
* Chicken (whole and thighs)
* Sausages/chorizo
* Cubed pancetta/bacon
* Peppers
* Eggs
* Butter
* Natural yogurt
* Cheese – Parmesan/strong Cheddar/goat's/mozzarella
* Pesto

**Freezer essentials**

* Frozen peas
* Readymade pastry

dry. I buy mine in 2kg (4lb) packs from the butcher or cash-and-carry and then freeze in individual 450g (1lb) blocks. If you have room you might want to keep minced pork and lamb as well for meatballs.

## Chicken (whole and thighs)

Always buy free range but don't worry about organic unless you know the supplier and the taste is worth it. Thanks to Jamie and Hugh everyone is far more aware of what mass-produced chicken involves. I know there is the counter argument about cost and families on tight budgets. For me that is a bad proposition. Causing an animal to suffer that kind of treatment so we can eat cheap food is fundamentally wrong. I knew that before I kept my own chickens but feel it even more strongly now. You can budget by buying whole chickens for a roast then using the carcass and bits for stock/sandwiches/salads so the entire bird gets used. Chicken thighs are relatively inexpensive. Buy them skinned and boned for easy cooking.

## Sausages/chorizo

Yet again I suggest you buy the best quality you can, and choose meat from outdoor pigs. The flavour and texture will all tell in the finished dish. Where I live in Sussex we are spoiled for choice with local butchers and farm shops, but supermarkets are improving their ranges too. I keep a selection of sausages in the fridge and freezer, plus one of my top ingredients, the cooking chorizo. A little cubed chorizo added to a pasta sauce or a chicken casserole (see page 58) is like a taste bomb.

## Cubed pancetta

Cubed pancetta (the Italian version of bacon) is always in my fridge in small packs for use in pasta, salad and soup dishes. I prefer its texture and smoky flavour to the lardons of bacon you can buy, which tend to be too big and meaty for these kinds of recipes – though they do work well in heartier stews or sauces for chicken. Cook pancetta in a pan with no added oil for little crispy cubes and add to salads such as the dish on page 68.

## Peppers

Red, yellow and orange – all good for adding colour, texture, useful vitamins and sweet flavour to everything from salads to stir-fries. The secret is to brown them really well, either in the oven, under a grill or in a pan so that the skins blacken and blister. That way the flesh loses any bitter flavour and becomes sweet and intense as the natural sugars caramelise. Younger children often dislike the skins so I introduced mine to peppers using the pasta dish on page 49. The peppers are skinned with a peeler and cooked until soft so that they almost disappear into the sauce. Look out for the elongated peppers called Romano – they are finer and sweeter. And keep a jar or two of shop-bought grilled peppers in olive oil in the store cupboard to use in a hurry.

## Eggs

Eggs are an ideal food: they make endless easy meals on their own but also transform so many cooking processes. Teach your children to make the basic egg dishes and they will be able to feed themselves in a hurry. Always buy free range. I don't actually store my eggs in the fridge as I don't like to cook with them cold – they don't tend to perform their magic so well – but I do have a fast turnover. Use older eggs for cakes and meringues; freeze leftover yolks and whites separately for meringues and sauces.

## Butter

Even through the decades of anti-dairy attitudes, I have never given up on butter. The alternative spreads you can buy have to be processed to make them solid and they don't taste very good to me. So it's back to the less is more approach: butter should be an occasional treat. In my opinion it is essential for baking. Keep a block in the freezer for emergencies.

## Natural yogurt

Great as an alternative to cream, for stirring into soups or curries, and using for dips. I find the no-fat version too thin so I buy a regular one but not the firmly set yogurt. (Try the yogurt and mango chutney mix for the salad on page 120.) Watch out for

Greek-style yogurt, which can contain as much fat as double cream (which is why it tastes so good!). Also beware of crème fraîche, which is basically the French version of double cream. For a similar flavour without the calories, go for soured cream instead.

## Cheese

For cooking I keep a selection of really good Parmesan, vintage Cheddar and buffalo mozzarella. As the children grew up I gradually bought better-quality cheese; when they were younger, they didn't notice the difference. The stronger the flavour of the cheese, the less you need to use when cooking, so find a balance between price and quality.

## Pesto

Homemade basil pesto is absolutely wonderful but there are countless ready-made versions available, both chilled and jars of longlife. Pesto from a jar can be rather chemical in flavour but good enough for emergencies. A good chilled pesto should be intensely fragrant with basil and just contain the key ingredients – basil, Parmesan, olive oil, pine nuts and garlic. Keep a tub or two in the fridge or freezer, and freeze leftover pesto from an opened carton in individual ice cube trays.

# Freezer essentials

## Frozen peas

Or in my freezer, petits pois, as I like their delicacy. Is there anyone of any age who doesn't like frozen peas? They are the essential accompaniment to cottage pie and perfect for all kinds of quick dishes (see the carbonara on page 53).

Pour peas into a pan of boiling water and return to the boil. Then drain and serve. Any leftovers can go into salads or pasta dishes. I also recommend you keep to hand frozen sweetcorn, mixed frozen veg and frozen chopped spinach. They are easier to use and much better nutritionally than fresh veg you have left hanging about in the bottom of the fridge.

## Readymade pastry

Until recently, apart from puff, readymade pastry was dull and lacking in flavour. But now you can get it made with butter, and what a difference. Taste and texture are excellent and make pastry dishes a possibility on a work night. I keep a range in the freezer – shortcrust, puff (even the ready-rolled sheets) and, though not made with butter, filo pastry.

# Buying and storing food

### How not to shop until you drop

Planning and good organisation are the two pillars on which I have built my working life (or tried to!), both at home and away from it. Time spent in advance is time halved when you are up and running, and this is as true in the kitchen as anywhere else. Nowadays we have the luxury of online ordering and flexible opening times but careful organisation and planning are still important.

### What kind of food should I buy?

I can't say it enough: aim to buy the best you can afford. Plan cheaper meals based on staple ingredients such as those you will find in this book and avoid waste. Cheap food is usually cheap for a reason: you can't cut corners without either the quality, the animal or the producer suffering – sometimes all three.

Local food in season is the best place to start your food shopping, for ethical, nutritional and economic reasons. There is no better time to support your local producers. And when you shop in the supermarket check what's on the label. In my opinion, if you don't understand what is on the label how can you be sure of what you are buying? Ask questions and research what you are buying.

### Budgeting

I'll say it again! The secret of good eating is to choose cheaper cuts but go for better quality. In fact, I recommend you feed the family like peasants. The

Mediterranean diet isn't just the healthiest; it is also delicious, as it's based on the best-quality, simple, everyday ingredients.

It's a bit like a fashion stylist's recommendations for a good wardrobe: buy a few expensive classics that will last and then learn to be clever with the accessories. My classics would be really good meat and fish, olive oil and Parmesan cheese, padded out with seasonal (so cheaper and better) fresh vegetables, pasta and rice.

## It says it serves four! You must be joking….

In a professional kitchen portion control is vital: you make much of your profit on ensuring there is no waste, while making sure your customers feel they are getting value for money. We need to manage the same trick at home, but it can be a challenge.

So with this book I have followed a strategy. Recipes for four serve the average family of two adults with two medium-sized children. If you are feeding hungry teenage boys (or active girls), then the recipes will probably do for two to three. Keep servings of meat and fish to between 100–175g (4–6oz) a head, pasta and rice 75–100g (3–4oz) a head, and the five fruit and veg a day should come to at least 450g (1lb) for adults. However, do remember small children need to eat a balanced diet for their stage of life. Adult diet regimes are not suitable for them – children are growing and need the right food to enable them to do so. Check with your doctor or a qualified nutritionist before putting a child on any kind of diet.

## Freezing and storing

I suggest as the main cook in the house you invest in a good all-round cookery book that explains all the basic methods and dishes. This should cover how to freeze, as I don't have room to go into too much detail here. My freezer is literally my treasure chest, particularly now there are so many more interesting and convenient frozen foods to buy. If you have a freezer it's worth investing in a small microwave oven for defrosting – particularly useful if you forget to take out ingredients in the morning to cook that evening.

Store dry food in airtight containers in cool dark cupboards (not next to the oven or freezer or by a sunny window) to keep them at their best. Learn which use-by dates to follow to eat safely – for example, nuts and oils go rancid and really unpleasant, flours can get weevils, while I find dried pasta just loses a bit of quality but is still edible.

## What is healthy eating?

Whatever the media's agenda, they manage to pile on the guilt just by the number of different research studies they report on. We bounce from one statistic to another. I try to shut out all the background noise when cooking and go back to my grandmother's maxims: a little of what you fancy does you good, and moderation in all things. Please note the two important words: little and moderation. My godfather, Neil, an old-fashioned GP, has always advised me that it's far better to make sure your diet is 80–90% good rather than beating yourself up about the 10% that isn't. So use common sense. Sugary drinks and sweets can all be eaten once in a while, but not as part of your everyday diet.

Our modern diets are far too full of over-processed foods, which by their nature are often high in salt, fat and sugar. These are added to give flavour or to bulk out inferior foods, to make foods easier to store for much longer – and because we have all got used to the high levels of processed flavour. Labelling is now so complex we really can't understand what it means. So I follow my own set of basic rules. I cook what I can myself when possible and if I do buy a readymade product, I check the label.

Too much salt is a real problem in modern diets. The guidelines are to eat less than 6g a day – that's a whole teaspoonful and some things you buy contain that in just one serving. But properly seasoned food tastes better, and if you make your own, you know just how much salt has gone in.

## Dealing with faddy eaters

Don't worry when children hit a fussy patch (which most will do at some time) – picture yourself as a calm smiling wall and don't allow mealtimes to become a battleground. My eldest daughter lived on tinned spaghetti hoops and fish fingers at every meal for six months when she was three and I just went with the flow. She got bored, decided she wanted a change and has eaten practically everything since.

### My rules for feeding my family are as follows:

- Simple, colourful, fresh and tasty
- Serve a rainbow – as many different colours as possible and try to exceed the five-a-day fruit and veg whenever possible
- Buy the best I can afford of cheaper foods
- Eat as wide a variety of fresh food as possible
- Mainly veg and carbohydrate with a little protein, fat and sugar
- Avoid processed food on the whole, but sometimes certain things are worth the time saving. (If you wonder what the definition of processed food is; sadly, on the whole, it's everything where the work has been done for you.)
- Keep on serving them things they don't like; apparently a child has to taste something 12 times before their taste buds grow accustomed to a new flavour. That's why we've all grown to eat things such as avocado and spinach that we hated as children
- Children really don't like dry food that's hard to swallow, which is why so many of them love roast lunches with good hot gravy

### Feeding vegetarians

Like increasing numbers of people I tend to eat a mainly vegetarian diet with some meat or fish two or three times a week and some meals with just a little meat added. It seems to make sense on all levels. So quite a large proportion of this book is vegetarian but with tips on adding meat if wanted. If you haven't had many dealings with vegetarians, check what level they are at: full vegetarians eat no flesh (meat or fish) at all and will avoid cheese made with animal rennet (that's most cheese you can buy easily). Watch out for hidden ingredients – such as fish in Worcestershire sauce.

### Manners – which battles are worth fighting?

Some are so worth the fight that not squaring up to them is a dereliction of parenting, while others have been a bit of a red herring. It is our job to teach our children skills for life, and eating well and healthily is one of the most important – they may not be grateful at the time but I can promise you they will thank you later.

Sitting down to eat together (at least once a fortnight) and banging on about table manners has finally reaped its reward. And as they grow up you learn a lot when you sit and eat together – particularly if they have friends round.

The other biggie worth the aggro is clearing the

table and loading the dishwasher. Remember, habits are the hardest thing to change, so aim to instil good ones at an early age. By spending a little time when they are smaller, you are saving serious work when they are older.

# Start cooking

**There's a little problem. I can't cook…**
Listen here, this is important! Cooking is a skill, like riding a bicycle or making a bed; if you learn how to do it properly and keep practising, you will get better and better at it (and quicker!). I promise you anyone can learn to cook. It's unusual in that it's both an art and a science. So it offers something for everyone. You might be a natural baker, a keen sauce maker or a lover of all things pasta – learn how to cook for yourself and the world is literally your oyster.

Sadly, one of the consequences of all the chefs on TV is that everyone has started to see cooking as a 'leisure activity' – complicated and needing lots of specialist knowledge and equipment. Well, that may be true of restaurant kitchens, but the cooking we do in our own kitchen is different.

So my suggestion is to start small. Even a boiled egg is a thing of wonder when served with Marmite

## Cooking tips

- All spoonfuls are level

- Cooking times and ovens. Ovens are like children – no two are the same. It's well worth finding out how yours performs. The classic test was to make and cook a batch of sponge fairy cakes using a standard recipe. If your batch cooks in 20 minutes or 10 instead of the expected 15 minutes, you need to adjust timings accordingly. Magazines get more complaints about baking recipes than any other kind – normally for this reason alone! (Another useful way to gauge your oven is to keep an eye on the time it takes to roast potatoes.)

- Imperial v. metric – stick with one set of measurements and don't jump between

- Dishes and tins – use the size specified or the timings will be different. I've tried to keep to just a couple of tins and baking dishes as they are the ones I use at home

- Raw or lightly cooked egg dishes should not be served to the very young, pregnant women, infirm or elderly people

soldiers made with really good bread. And give yourself a little time. Learn from your mistakes… everyone makes them (and sometimes the mistakes end up better than the original). When you first cook something, follow the recipe carefully before heading off piste. The writer has used his/her experience to come up with what they think works best. When you understand the process and what the dish should taste like, then have a go at adapting it.

### Timing

When you try a new recipe, allow yourself extra time and read the method properly before you begin. Get everything listed in the ingredients out on to the work surface. Then start cooking.

My recipes have all been tested by someone else, too, and they have checked the timings. I tend to cook them faster than it says: I trained as a cook, I've been cooking for a long time (and used to run a professional kitchen catering for over 40 every day) – but you may take longer. Don't put yourself under pressure: cooking should be enjoyable and that will happen as you gain in confidence and skill.

# Basic equipment

Good kitchen equipment should last a lifetime. When you think how much use you will be getting from it, then it really is worth buying the best you can afford. My tip is to buy your equipment in the sales. Avoid gimmicks and gadgets that simply take up space in your cupboards and are usually awful to wash-up.

### My freezer

I really cannot overstate the importance of the freezer in feeding my family conveniently and well. Freezing techniques and packaging have improved beyond measure since I started cooking and there are some really innovative ideas in the supermarkets and farm shops. If planning a new purchase, go for a size that gives you the flexibility to feed your family for a week in an emergency.

### My fridge

As above, the largest and most efficient you can manage to fit in the kitchen.

### The microwave

A small one for defrosting (especially bread), melting chocolate, softening butter, etc.

### Hand-held blender

My desert-island tool. Mine is a professional caterer's version with a really strong motor and sharp blades. I use it all the time for blending soups in the pan and making batters, hummus and sauces. They are also wonderful for puréeing baby food. Get one with the little nut/spice blender attachment for making small amounts of breadcrumbs, spice mixes and pesto.

### Hand-held electric mixer

Unless you are a really serious baker (and I am a fairly serious one!), I would avoid one of those wonderful freestanding, all singing and dancing mixers. They take up too much space, need a lot of washing and actually I find I can do just as well with my little hand-held version, creaming cakes, whisking up meringues or making mayonnaise.

### Knives (and a good chopping board)

Cheap knives go blunt fast and are often hard to hold properly so it is far easier to cut yourself. I still use the carbon-steel knife set I got at Leith's cookery school. Ask a good butcher to show you how to sharpen them or search on the internet.

### Utensils

Choose well-made stainless-steel classics – the handles are longer lasting.

### Pans – non stick and well made

The easiest way to cut the amount of fat you use in cooking is to use a good non-stick frying pan. With the best ones you can cook without any oil at all. A good set of pans is an investment for life – I have a selection of sizes with well-fitting lids. Plus, I find a stock pan useful for boiling pasta for large numbers.

# family
# essentials

According to recent research most mums in the UK have a basic repertoire of just nine recipes that they rely on to feed their families. Even as a food writer I know I still return to the same old favourites again and again – they are almost hard-wired into my brain so I can make them on autopilot after a busy day. What's more, I know I've always got the ingredients to hand, and most important, everyone will eat them.

The main aim of this book is to add more options to those nine recipes, so I am kicking off with my own essential 12 – you could call them the definitive dozen! Yes, there's a fairly classic chilli and a spaghetti Bolognese in here, as I think they are the best of their class, but also some twists on old favourites to tempt you off the beaten path.

These recipes are, by definition, comfort food but they are also well-balanced and healthy options that satisfy my desire to serve a real meal but quickly, enjoyably and without too much work. And another bonus is, if you learn how to cook these well, you will have picked up a set of basic cooking skills that you will use again and again. ⟶

# 1 Anything goes veggie cashew-nut stir-fry

Stir-fries are a great way to introduce the family to what I call 'vegetables by the back door'. My children have all had their fussy moments and my strategy is to keep things calm (and occasionally use subterfuge) and serve a stir-fry with a range of veg in, trying to give everyone something they like and including cashew nuts, which they all seem to enjoy. I grant an amnesty so any personal horrors can be picked out by the individual concerned, as long as they eat the rest. In this way I keep serving a selection of vegetables and have found that even the pickiest diners gradually try – and enjoy – previously scorned items such as courgette and even sprouts. You can also add cubes of chicken, salmon or tofu, depending what you have to hand or the ingredient in favour at the time.

⟶ Serve with plain rice.

---

*Serves 3–4*
*Prepare 20 minutes*
*Cook 8–10 minutes*

650g–1kg (1¼–2¼lb) colourful
    vegetables – I always try to include
    broccoli, carrots, peppers and
    mushrooms, then, depending on
    what is in the fridge, I might add
    leek, green beans, mangetout,
    cauliflower, shredded cabbage
    or kale
1 tbsp tomato ketchup
1 tbsp dark brown muscovado sugar
2 tbsp soy sauce
2 tbsp groundnut oil
1 small red onion, sliced
1 clove garlic, chopped
2.5cm (1in) fresh root ginger, peeled
    and finely chopped
100g (4oz) unsalted natural cashew
    nuts

1 Cut all the vegetables into similar-sized pieces about 3.5cm (1½in) square, discarding any seeds, peel, skin, etc. Mix the ketchup, sugar and soy together in a small bowl or ramekin.

2 Heat the oil in a wok or large frying pan until smoking hot and add the onion, garlic and ginger. Stir-fry for a minute until golden then add the vegetables and fry over a high heat for 3–4 minutes till they start to colour. Add the soy mixture and cashew nuts and stir for another minute or so till the vegetables are just tender.

*Busy mum's lifesaver* For non veggies, add about 350g (12oz) chicken or salmon cut into 2.5cm (1in) cubes and fry in a tablespoon of oil for 3–4 minutes until just cooked through before cooking the vegetables. Remove from the pan then return with the soy mixture at the end. Keep a useful pack of ready-chopped root ginger in the freezer for real convenience.

# 2 Rosti-topped fish pie

Another essential recipe that confirms my belief that fussier children will eat things they normally reject if served with plenty of tasty sauce and something with a crunchy texture. So this sauce is very creamy and the rosti topping avoids problems for those who dislike the dryness of mashed potato.

➡ Serve with steamed broccoli and sugar snap peas.

*Serves 4–6*
*Prepare 30 minutes*
*Cook 1 hour*

450ml (¾ pint) semi-skimmed milk
150ml (¼ pint) single cream (optional but nice – use more milk instead)
450g (1lb) firm white fish fillet such as cod or haddock
230g (8oz) undyed smoked haddock fillet
2 bay leaves
2 large free-range eggs, hard-boiled, peeled and roughly chopped
75g (3oz) butter
50g (2oz) plain flour
4 tbsp chopped flat-leaf parsley
1.25kg (2½lb) medium waxy potatoes such as Charlotte, scrubbed and halved
salt, freshly ground black pepper and freshly grated nutmeg

1 Preheat the oven to 200°C/fan oven 180°C/Gas Mark 6. Put the milk, cream if using, cod and smoked haddock in a large roasting tin with the bay leaves. Cover with foil and cook in the oven for 10–12 minutes until the fish is just cooked through and no longer translucent – it should break into flakes. Lift the fish on to a plate and reserve the liquid. Discard the bay leaf. Break the fish into large chunks, discarding skin and bones. Arrange the fish over the base of a shallow 1.75 litre (3 pint) ovenproof dish. Scatter over the eggs.

2 Melt 50g (2oz) butter in a pan and add the flour and cook for a minute. Off the heat, gradually add the cooking liquid from the fish a few tablespoons at a time, stirring in each addition and keeping the sauce smooth. Return to the heat and bring to the boil, stirring all the time; then simmer for 5 minutes, stirring occasionally. Off the heat, stir in the parsley and season with nutmeg, salt and pepper. Pour over the fish and leave to cool.

3 Cook the potatoes in a large pan of boiling water for 5 minutes. Drain and leave till cool enough to handle. Grate on a large grater. Melt the remaining butter in a small pan and mix with the grated potato and plenty of seasoning. Spoon over the fish to completely cover. Cook the fish pie for 35–40 minutes until golden brown and crisp on top.

*Busy mum's lifesaver* **Add cooked prawns or sautéed sliced leeks to the fish for added interest.**

# 3 Roast honey and cumin chicken

This is an easy but satisfying roast that makes its own delicious gravy. I find it ideal for the first night of any family holiday here in Britain that involves a long drive – for us that's usually Cornwall for the surfing or the west coast of Scotland. I pop the chicken into its marinade in a bag before we leave home, then put it into a cold bag. When we arrive exhausted (but excited) at the other end, it goes straight into the oven with scrubbed potatoes to bake.

⟶ Serve with salad or peas. Follow with chocolate brownies (recipe page 197) and vanilla ice cream picked up at the local shop, and everyone is happy.

---

*Serves 4*
*Prepare 10 minutes plus 15 minutes marinating*
*Cook 1¼ hours*

2 tbsp olive oil
2 tbsp clear honey
2 tsp ground cumin
2 cloves garlic, crushed
1 tbsp red wine vinegar
1 large free-range chicken, about 2kg (4lb)
salt and freshly ground black pepper

1 Preheat the oven to 220°C/fan oven 200°C/Gas Mark 7. Mix together the oil, honey, cumin, garlic and vinegar with seasoning. Pour over the chicken and leave to marinate for 15 minutes (up to an hour if you have time).

2 Remove the chicken from the marinade. Stand it in a roasting tin and pour over 150ml (¼ pint) water and roast in the oven for 15 minutes. Reduce the oven temperature to 190°C/fan oven 170°C/Gas Mark 5 for a further hour, basting regularly. Remove from the oven and leave to stand for 10 minutes. Carve and serve.

*Busy mum's lifesaver* Cook halved new potatoes scattered with chopped fresh rosemary around the chicken for an all-in-one easy roast.

# 4 Easy Thai vegetable and coconut curry

This curry is quick and simple – I make it when there are plenty of vegetables in the fridge.
The more colourful the better, so aim for orange, purple, yellow, red and a whole range of greens.
Use a top-quality curry paste – comparing the ingredients label to a good recipe will give you
an idea of what you are buying.

➡ Serve with wedges of lime and steamed Thai rice.

*Serves 4*
*Prepare 15 minutes*
*Cook 15 minutes*

2–4 tbsp good-quality Thai green
    curry paste
400ml can coconut milk
450g (1lb) butternut squash, peeled,
    seeded and cubed
1 head broccoli, trimmed and cut
    into florets
1 red pepper, seeded and sliced
100g (4oz) frozen peas
4 salad onions onions, sliced
4 tbsp fresh coriander, roughly
    chopped
juice of 1 lime
1 tbsp light brown muscovado sugar
    or palm sugar

1 Heat the curry paste with the coconut milk in a medium saucepan
until simmering. Add the squash and simmer for 8–10 minutes or
until just tender. Add the broccoli, peppers and peas (and cubed fish
or chicken if using, see below) and simmer for 3–4 minutes or until
the vegetables are cooked through.

2 Stir in the salad onions, coriander, lime juice and sugar, and serve,
spooned over bowls of rice.

*Busy mum's lifesaver* Add 350g (12oz) cubed firm white
fish fillets, salmon or chicken breasts with the squash. Branded curry
pastes come in different strengths; choose one your family will like.

# 5 Crunchy-topped chicken and broccoli gratin

This is my version of a Sixties classic (I think it was known as Chicken Divan) – cooked chicken and broccoli layered with a creamy sauce and topped with crumbs and baked. There are all kinds of versions in existence – some rather dodgy Seventies ones use mayonnaise or even condensed mushroom soup. I like a lightly curried béchamel sauce and if I have time – at the weekend, for example – I poach a whole chicken as suggested here, and use the stock for my sauce. I also leave the chicken to cool completely in its cooking liquid. Steam rather than boil the broccoli for the best flavour and colour.

➡ Serve with new potatoes.

---

*Serves 4*
*Prepare 25 minutes*
*Cook 1 hour 35 minutes if poaching chicken from scratch*

1.35kg (3lb) free-range chicken
stock flavourings: an onion, carrot, stick of celery, cut into chunks; plus 2 bay leaves, 6–8 black peppercorns, a sprig of fresh thyme and a large pinch of salt
450g (1lb) broccoli, cut into florets
65g (2½oz) butter
50g (2oz) plain flour
1 tbsp medium curry powder
450ml (¾ pint) semi-skimmed milk
4 tbsp grated Parmesan
50g (2oz) white breadcrumbs
large pinch cayenne pepper

1 Put the chicken in a saucepan with the stock flavourings and enough water to just cover. Bring to the boil, cover and simmer very gently for 50–60 minutes until the juices run clear when the chicken is pierced with a skewer. Cool the chicken in the liquid and then remove and take the flesh off the bone. Discard the skin and arrange the chicken meat in the bottom of a 1.75 litre (3 pint) ovenproof dish. Keep the liquid that the chicken was cooked in.

2 Preheat the oven to 200°C/fan oven 180°C/ Gas Mark 6. Steam the broccoli over a pan of simmering water for 3–4 minutes until just tender. Arrange over the chicken. Melt 50g (2oz) butter in a medium pan and stir in the flour and curry powder. Off the heat gradually whisk in the milk and 150ml (¼ pint) cooking liquid from the chicken. Return to the heat, bring to the boil and stir until thickened. Simmer for 5 minutes stirring occasionally. Season to taste and stir in the Parmesan. Spoon over the broccoli.

3 Mix together the breadcrumbs and cayenne pepper. Sprinkle over the top of the bake and dot with the remaining butter. Bake for 20–25 minutes until golden and bubbling.

*Busy mum's lifesaver* Use leftover roast chicken or bought cooked chicken instead and substitute a readymade cheese sauce from the supermarket for the béchamel. Freeze any leftover chicken stock for soups and other dishes.

# 6 The best Bolognese

This recipe has evolved over the years; it started life from the recipe in *The Classic Italian Cookbook* by Marcella Hazan, one of my cookery bibles. I make a batch every month or so and freeze it in individual portions so that I can defrost as much as I need (in the microwave if in a hurry). It means there's always a quick and satisfying meal for one or more on standby, and the children and I rely on its constant presence in the freezer.

➡ Serve with spaghetti or linguine. I cook 75–100g (3–4oz) dry weight a head.

---

*Serves 6–8*
*Prepare 20 minutes*
*Cook up to 2½ hours*

1 tbsp olive oil
1 medium onion, finely chopped
1 large carrot, finely diced
2 sticks celery, finely chopped
2 cloves garlic, crushed
500g (1lb 2oz) good-quality beef
   mince
200ml (7floz) dry white wine
200ml (7floz) semi-skimmed milk
freshly grated nutmeg
2 x 400g cans Italian plum tomatoes
salt and freshly ground black pepper

1 Heat the oil in a large non-stick sauté pan. Add the onion, carrot, celery and garlic and cook over a low heat for 5 minutes until softened but not browned. Turn up the heat, add the beef mince and season well. Break up the mince with a fork and stir it until lightly browned.

2 Add the wine and simmer fast until almost evaporated, then add the milk and grated nutmeg and do the same. Stir in the canned tomatoes, breaking them up with the edge of the spoon. Season and bring to the boil. Simmer so the surface is just bubbling slightly at the edges. Half cover the pan and simmer for at least 1½ hours and up to 2½ hours if time, until the liquid is reduced and the sauce is thick and tomatoey. Add more water if the sauce dries out too much and stir occasionally.

3 Check the seasoning and serve with spaghetti or linguine, or cool and freeze for up to three months. I freeze it in leftover small pasta sauce or pesto pots from the supermarket, washed out first, of course.

*Busy mum's lifesaver* There are no short cuts worth taking with this – in fact I go the other way in the winter and cook the sauce overnight in the slow oven of the Aga. Slow cookers work just as well. Follow the recipe and make the sauce in a sauté pan, then pour it into the slow cooker to carry on cooking while you're at work. The result is a wonderful intense sauce, so you don't need to serve as much with the pasta and the dish goes further.

# 7 Leek-topped cottage pie

The perfect comfort dish but one that creates debate about what should and shouldn't go in. Some of my family insist on the addition of baked beans (as in the version my mother always served), while I swear by tomato ketchup and lots of fresh parsley. I also like the leek and swede topping; the finished effect is less stodgy than plain mash and it's yet another way to introduce extra vegetables on to the plate.

⟶ Serve with peas or broccoli.

-------------------------------------------------------------------

*Serves 4*
*Prepare 20 minutes*
*Cook 1 hour*

1 tbsp olive oil
1 medium onion, finely chopped
1 medium carrot, finely chopped
500g (1lb 2oz) good-quality beef
   mince
1–2 tbsp Worcestershire sauce
2 tbsp tomato ketchup
4–5 tbsp chopped flat-leaf parsley
500ml (14floz) beef stock (from a
   cube)
650g (1¼lb) old potatoes, peeled
   and cubed
1 large swede, peeled and cubed
40g (1½oz) butter
2 medium leeks, thinly sliced
50g (2oz) vintage Cheddar, grated
salt and freshly ground black pepper

1 Preheat the oven to 200°C/fan oven 180°C/Gas Mark 6. Heat the oil in a large non-stick frying pan or sauté pan and cook the onion and carrot for 3 minutes until softened. Add the mince and break up with a fork. Fry for a few minutes until lightly browned. Stir in the Worcestershire sauce, ketchup and parsley. Add the stock and seasoning and bring to the boil. Simmer half covered for 25–30 minutes, stirring occasionally. Transfer to a 1.75 litre (3 pint) shallow ovenproof dish.

2 While the mince is cooking, place the potatoes and swede in a pan with enough cold water to just cover. Bring to the boil and simmer for 15–20 minutes until tender. Meanwhile heat the butter in a frying pan and add the leeks. Cook for 5 minutes until softened and starting to brown.

3 Drain the potatoes and swede thoroughly, return to the pan and mash until smooth – add a little milk if the mixture is dry – then mix in the leeks with any melted butter. Season well and spoon over the top of the mince mixture. Rough up the surface with a fork then scatter with the cheese. Bake for 25–30 minutes until golden and bubbling.

*Busy mum's lifesaver* Make double quantities and freeze as individual pies in foil containers from the supermarket.

# 8 Mark's chilli

This chilli recipe is quick and easy to make after work and I usually have all the ingredients to hand. I try to take some mince out of the freezer in the morning but if I forget, I resort to the microwave when I get in from work. It's my daughters' father's recipe – he's a great cook.

➡ Serve with rice and peas or – my stepson's personal choice – with soured cream, grated Cheddar and shredded lettuce, all wrapped in a warm tortilla.

*Serves 4–6*
*Prepare 20 minutes*
*Cook 50 minutes*

1 tbsp olive oil
1 large onion, finely chopped
2 cloves garlic, finely chopped
500g (1lb 2oz) good-quality beef mince
2 tsp ground cumin
1 tsp smoked paprika
1–2 tsp chilli powder (depending on family preferred heat levels)
1 tbsp dried oregano
3 tbsp tomato purée
600ml (1 pint) beef stock (made from a cube)
2 x 400g cans red kidney beans, drained and rinsed
salt and freshly ground black pepper

1 Heat the oil in a large sauté pan or non-stick deep frying pan and cook the onion and garlic for 3 minutes until softened but not browned. Add the mince, break up with a spoon and fry until lightly browned. Stir in the cumin, smoked paprika, chilli and oregano and cook for a minute, then add the tomato purée and stir well. Pour in the stock and seasoning and bring to the boil. Half cover the pan with a lid and simmer gently for 30–40 minutes until the liquid is reduced by half, stirring occasionally.

2 Stir in the drained beans, bring to the boil and simmer uncovered for a further 5 minutes. Check seasoning and serve.

*Busy mum's lifesaver* Make the chilli in advance and store it in the fridge in a covered container for up to three days. Any dish with spices in will develop in flavour and taste even better a day or so later.

# 9 The best ever lasagne

The secret to good lasagne is a really well-flavoured Bolognese, spread thinly so you don't end up with too much meat but a satisfyingly unctuous blend of meat sauce, pasta and creamy béchamel. I teach this version to students on my cooking courses to demonstrate a range of useful cookery skills, from chopping an onion to making a lump-free béchamel (aka white) sauce. It's also the dish my girls used to request for the night before a new term started at school – eaten as a special-treat supper on trays in front of a girlie movie, followed by chocolate cookies-and-cream ice cream.

→ Serve with a salad.

*Serves 6–8*
*Prepare 25 minutes*
*Cook 40 minutes*

75g (3oz) butter, plus extra for
    greasing
75g (3oz) plain flour
1 litre (1¾ pint) semi-skimmed milk
1 amount Bolognese sauce –
    see page 30
200g (7oz) dried lasagne
50g (2oz) freshly grated Parmesan
salt and freshly ground black pepper

1 Preheat the oven to 200°C/fan oven 180°C/Gas Mark 6. Butter a large rectangular ovenproof dish that holds 2.5 litres (4 pints). To make the béchamel sauce, melt the butter in a medium non-stick pan then stir in the flour and cook over a low heat, stirring, for at least a minute. Remove the pan from the heat and gradually stir in the milk a few tablespoons at a time, keeping the mixture smooth. When all the milk has been added put the pan back on a medium heat and bring the sauce to the boil, stirring all the time. Simmer gently for a further couple of minutes until the thickness of thin cream, then season generously.

2 Spoon a little of the Bolognese sauce over the base of the dish to just cover and add spoonfuls of béchamel sauce. Cover with a single layer of lasagne. Spread with enough Bolognese sauce to barely cover the pasta then spread with a thin layer of béchamel. Sprinkle with grated Parmesan. Continue layering up the sauces, Parmesan and the pasta and finish with a layer of pasta topped with béchamel. Sprinkle with Parmesan.

3 Bake for 35–40 minutes until a golden crust forms on the top and the pasta is tender when pierced with a knife. Remove from the oven and leave to stand for 5 minutes before serving.

# 10 Cauliflower macaroni cheese

A marriage of two old favourites that (unsurprisingly) works really well – it adds a useful vegetable to one basic dish and transforms the other from a side vegetable to a main course. I sometimes replace half the cauliflower with broccoli. The secret is to drain the vegetables really thoroughly as cauliflower can hold on to a surprising amount of liquid, which then makes for a watery sauce.

→ Serve with peas if you feel like another vegetable.

*Serves 4*
*Prepare 15 minutes*
*Cook 35 minutes*

300g (10oz) macaroni
1 large cauliflower, trimmed and cut
   into florets
50g (2oz) butter
50g (2oz) plain flour
750ml (1¼ pints) semi-skimmed milk
100g (4oz) vintage Cheddar, grated
2 tsp Dijon mustard
2 tbsp white breadcrumbs
2 tbsp grated Parmesan
salt and freshly ground black pepper

1 Preheat the oven to 200°C/fan oven 180°C/ Gas Mark 6. Cook the pasta in plenty of boiling water for 8–10 minutes until just tender. Either cook the cauliflower in a separate pan of boiling water or place the cauliflower in a steamer or covered sieve and set over the pasta for the last 5 minutes until almost tender. Drain the pasta and arrange in a 1.75 litre (3 pint) ovenproof baking dish with the cooked cauliflower.

2 To make the sauce, melt the butter in a medium non-stick pan and stir in the flour. Cook for a minute stirring, then off the heat gradually whisk in the milk, keeping the mixture smooth. Return the pan to the heat and stir constantly until thickened. Simmer for 2 minutes, stirring. Off the heat stir in the Cheddar, mustard and seasoning. Pour over the pasta and vegetables to coat.

3 Mix the breadcrumbs and Parmesan and sprinkle over the dish. Cook in the oven for 25–30 minutes until the top is crisp and golden. Serve.

*Busy mum's lifesaver* Add halved cherry tomatoes cut-side up around the edge of the dish, before topping with the crumb mixture, to add colour. Use a really strong Cheddar to give the right kick then you won't need to use as much cheese, which helps keep the saturated fat content down.

# 11 Maple syrup and mustard-glazed sausage, red onion and potato roast

Perfect for a family supper, this is a really simple dish that makes the most of the wonderful coarse meaty texture and intense flavour of good locally produced sausages.

➡ Serve with seasonal vegetables such as runner beans or shredded Savoy cabbage.

---

*Serves 3–4*
*Prepare 15 minutes*
*Cook 45 minutes*

450g (1lb) your favourite pork
   sausages
2 medium red onions, cut into chunks
500g (1lb 2oz) small to medium-sized
   potatoes, scrubbed and quartered
2 tbsp maple syrup
1 tbsp grainy mustard
2 tbsp olive oil
2 tbsp chopped fresh thyme
salt and freshly ground black pepper

1 Preheat the oven to 200°C/ fan oven 180°C/Gas Mark 6. Twist the sausages in the middle then snip with scissors to create two smaller sausages. Place the sausages, onions and potatoes in a roasting tin so they fit in a tightly packed single layer. Mix together the maple syrup, mustard, oil and seasoning and pour over the ingredients in the tin. Scatter with the chopped thyme and mix well.

2 Roast for 40–45 minutes, turning occasionally, until the sausages are cooked through and the potatoes are crisp and golden.

*Busy mum's lifesaver* Use waxy or floury potatoes: both work well but gives a different finish. Just use what you have to hand. Try honey instead of maple syrup for a change.

# 12 Spiced lentil and vegetable soup

A winter lunch standby; I often make up a batch and keep it in the fridge for all comers. It also freezes well, improving in flavour with keeping, and it's great in a flask for packed lunches. It always goes down well on Bonfire Night.

→ Serve in mugs, with bread rolls or baked potatoes.

*Serves 4*
*Prepare 15 minutes*
*Cook 30 minutes*

2 tbsp olive oil
1 large onion, sliced
2 sticks celery, sliced
2 carrots, sliced
1 large leek, sliced
175g (6oz) red lentils
4–6 cloves
1 tbsp tomato purée
1.2 litres (2 pints) chicken stock (see right) or vegetable stock
large dash Worcestershire sauce
salt and freshly ground black pepper

1 Heat the oil in a large pan and add the onion, celery, carrots and leek. Cook over a low heat for 3–4 minutes until soft but not browned. Stir in the lentils, cloves, tomato purée, stock and seasoning. Bring to the boil and simmer gently for 20 minutes until the lentils are tender.

2 Whiz in a blender, or use a hand-held blender, until smooth. Reheat and stir in the Worcestershire sauce. Check seasoning and serve in warmed thick china mugs.

*Busy mum's lifesaver* Use homemade chicken stock if you've made some (see page 28) – you'll really notice the difference. To use, remove from the freezer the night before or if in a hurry defrost gently in a pan over a low heat.

# fast and fabulous pasta

I do worry that I cook far too much pasta, but when it is so easy, quick and delicious it can be hard not to. Who needs so-called convenience foods when, with a pack of pasta and a few store-cupboard ingredients you can have a far superior (and far cheaper) meal on the table in the time it takes to set the microwave, open the fiddly packaging and read the instructions? Just try the first recipe in this chapter and see what I mean. As I've said elsewhere, the more you cook these dishes, the more adept you will become. So keep practising. And remember most pasta dishes (apart from those with white sauce, such as the cauliflower macaroni cheese version on page 36) turn into great salads the next day. I've given a guide to pasta cooking times in each recipe, but always check the pack instructions as different brands do vary.

I follow the Italian practice of serving a lot of pasta with a smaller amount of sauce – for both economic and health reasons. Use a really good-quality pasta made in Italy with durum wheat – that is what Italian mums buy and serve their families. They usually make fresh pasta at home only for special occasions, as the good dried varieties are such excellent quality. →

# The essential tomato sauce

This recipe is straight out of the store cupboard and is what I cook when there is nothing else in the house. It comes out in emergencies when a group needs feeding in a hurry and I add whatever is to hand for variety. It's a godsend for that strange dead time between Christmas and New Year when you are bored with cooking and need to fill the children up. I never used to tell them that the sauce contained anchovies – they would all have pulled a face and refused to eat – but used this way they add a depth of flavour that gives the sauce its intensity. It also makes a perfect tomato topping for pizzas and is worth making in bulk and freezing in small potfuls as a base for all kinds of dishes.

→ To serve, toss with spaghetti and add a drizzle of extra-virgin olive oil if you feel like it.

---

*Serves 4–6*
*Prepare 10 minutes*
*Cook 15 minutes*

2 tbsp olive oil
2 cloves garlic, finely chopped
3–4 anchovy fillets, finely chopped
3–4 tbsp chopped flat-leaf parsley or
  fresh basil (optional)
400g can Italian plum tomatoes
300–400g (10–14oz) spaghetti
salt and freshly ground black pepper
freshly grated Parmesan, to serve

1 Heat the oil in a medium pan and add the garlic. Stir over a medium heat for 30 seconds but don't let it brown, then add the anchovies (and parsley if using) and cook for a further minute, stirring. Stir in the canned tomatoes with their juice, break up with a spoon and season. Simmer uncovered for 12–15 minutes, stirring regularly until thickened.

2 While the sauce is cooking bring a large pan of salted water to the boil, add the pasta and stir once. Cook according to packet instructions until al dente (that means tender, with a little texture, not soft and flabby). Drain and return to the pan, then add the sauce and toss together thoroughly. Serve with Parmesan.

*Busy mum's lifesaver* Add any of the following to the cooked sauce and heat through before tossing with the pasta:

● 200g can tuna in olive oil, drained and flaked

● 1 large aubergine, thinly sliced and fried in a little oil until golden

● 50g (2oz) stoned black olives and capers

● steamed broccoli florets

# Broccoli, anchovy and walnut pasta

Another easy last-minute supper dish that I make when I can't think of anything else. It's good with any kind of broccoli but particularly purple sprouting for its special flavour, or use a mix of cauliflower and broccoli together.

Serves 4
*Prepare 10 minutes*
*Cook 10 minutes*

350g (12oz) pasta shells
450g (1lb) purple sprouting broccoli,
    cut into short lengths
1 tbsp olive oil
4–6 anchovy fillets, chopped
¼ tsp dried chilli flakes
50g (2oz) walnut pieces, roughly
    chopped
grated rind of 1 lemon
salt and freshly ground black pepper
freshly grated Parmesan, to serve

1 Cook the pasta in a large pan of boiling water for 8–10 minutes until just tender. While the pasta is cooking, steam the broccoli over the pasta for 3–5 minutes until just tender. Drain the pasta and return to the pan.

2 Heat the oil in a medium frying pan, add the anchovy fillets and chilli flakes and cook for a minute. Stir in the broccoli, walnuts, lemon rind and seasoning. Add the broccoli mixture to the pasta and toss all together. Serve on warmed plates with grated Parmesan.

*Busy mum's lifesaver* As a special treat, try the Italian habit of using extra-virgin olive oil as a condiment. Just use a splash in all kinds of pasta dishes: add it when you toss the pasta and sauce together.

# Spaghetti with courgette and chilli

Make this dish with the smallest courgettes you can get: they are at their best when finger length – either from the supermarket or if you are lucky, from the farmer's market, garden or a window box. This is a family favourite that came originally from my ex-sister-in-law and is really easy to cook, for just yourself alone or up the quantities for more. Allow 75g (3oz) pasta and 1 small courgette per person.

*Serves 2–3*
*Prepare 5 minutes*
*Cook 10 minutes*

175–230g (6–8oz) spaghetti
1 tbsp extra-virgin olive oil
2 small courgettes, trimmed then
   halved lengthways and sliced
   thinly
1–2 cloves garlic, finely chopped
¼ tsp crushed dried chillies
salt and freshly ground black pepper
freshly grated Parmesan, to serve

1 Bring a large pan of water to the boil, add the spaghetti and cook for 10–12 minutes until just tender.

2 While the pasta is cooking, heat the oil in a medium frying pan and add the sliced courgettes in a single layer. Cook on a medium to high heat for 5–6 minutes until golden brown, turning to cook both sides. Add the garlic and chilli and cook for a further minute. Season the courgettes.

3 Drain the pasta and toss with the courgettes and any oil from the pan. Check seasoning and serve with freshly grated Parmesan.

*Busy mum's lifesaver* Add cubed pancetta to the courgette for a non-vegetarian alternative. Grated lemon zest tastes wonderful too.

# Roasted pepper, aubergine and chorizo pasta bake

The perfect summer family supper dish served simply with a salad. It's even good cold, taken to the beach for a picnic. This cheap and cheerful version uses budget chorizo and mozzarella but when I feel like I need a treat, I use a really good cooking chorizo and buffalo milk cheese. Leave out the chorizo for a vegetarian version.

*Serves 4*
*Prepare 20 minutes*
*Cook 45 minutes*

2 red Romano peppers, seeded and thickly sliced
1 medium aubergine, sliced lengthways
2 tbsp olive oil
230g (8oz) mini cooking chorizo sausages, halved
1 clove garlic, finely chopped
8–10 leaves fresh basil, shredded
400g can chopped Italian tomatoes
350g (12oz) fusilli pasta
100g (4oz) mozzarella, torn into pieces
3–4 tbsp grated Parmesan
salt and freshly ground black pepper

1 Preheat the oven to 200°C/fan oven 180°C/Gas Mark 6. Brush the sliced peppers and aubergine with half the oil, season and place in a single layer in a roasting tin with the chorizo. Cook in the oven for 20–25 minutes, turning once, until charred and cooked through.

2 While the vegetables and chorizo are roasting, heat the remaining oil in a medium pan, add the garlic and half the shredded basil and cook for 30 seconds. Add the canned tomatoes and simmer over a medium heat for 10 minutes, stirring occasionally, to give a thick sauce. Season to taste.

3 Meanwhile cook the pasta in boiling water for 12 minutes or according to pack instructions; drain and mix with the tomato sauce. Cut the cooked peppers and aubergine into strips and stir into the pasta with the chorizo and mozzarella. Transfer to a 2 litre (3½ pint) oiled shallow ovenproof dish and scatter with the remaining basil and Parmesan. Bake for 15–20 minutes until the top is golden.

# Pasta and borlotti bean soup

There are variations of pasta and pulse soups all over Italy and this is one of my favourites. It comes from my friend Gianni, the owner of my wonderful local Italian deli in Tunbridge Wells. I buy my dried pasta, Italian sausage and great pesto from him and we share recipes over a cappuccino. Most of his come from his mother at home in Calabria in southern Italy and are made with really good basic simple ingredients. His tip with this soup is to prepare it up to the end of the second step then cook the pasta separately and toss it with some olive oil. Keep the pasta covered in the fridge with the soup in a separate container. When someone needs a fast meal, heat the soup and stir in a handful of the cooked pasta and extra borlotti beans. The texture will be far better than if you cook the soup with the pasta and leave it all to sit in the pot – the pasta will swell and go soggy.

*Serves 4–6*
*Prepare 15 minutes*
*Cook 35 minutes*

1 tbsp olive oil
1 small onion, finely chopped
1 stalk celery, sliced
1 small carrot, diced
2 cloves garlic, chopped
1 sprig fresh rosemary, chopped
200g can chopped Italian tomatoes
2 x 400g cans borlotti beans
100g (4oz) soup pasta or small pasta shapes
salt and freshly ground black pepper
extra-virgin olive oil, to serve
freshly grated Parmesan, to serve

1 Heat the oil in a heavy-based pan, add the onion, celery, carrot and garlic and cook over a low heat for 5 minutes until softened. Add the rosemary, chopped tomatoes, 100ml (4floz) water and seasoning, bring to the boil and simmer gently for 10 minutes until the liquid is reduced and you have a thick sauce.

2 Add 1 can of the borlotti beans and their juices to the pan and cook for a further 3–4 minutes. Purée coarsely with a hand-held blender or mash with a vegetable masher. Add 600ml (1pint) water and bring to the boil.

3 Add the pasta, bring back to the boil and simmer vigorously for 8–10 minutes, stirring once or twice, until the pasta is tender. Drain the remaining borlotti beans and stir in for the last 3–4 minutes, adding extra water if necessary. Check seasoning. Spoon into warm serving bowls and serve with extra-virgin olive oil for drizzling and grated Parmesan.

*Busy mum's lifesaver* If you don't have special soup pasta (my children call it doll's pasta), break spaghetti or other long pasta into short pieces – or use the smallest pasta shape you have in the cupboard and cook according to pack instructions.

# Farfalle with sage-roasted squash and goat's cheese

Hurray for roasted butternut squash – here it makes a colourful autumn pasta dish that is great served cold the next day as a salad. You can tell butternut squash is a family favourite as it pops up in all kinds of dishes in this book – and it's bound to be a hit with your children too. Try making this recipe with cubed feta instead of goat's cheese for a change.

*Serves 4*
*Prepare 15 minutes*
*Cook 35 minutes*

1 medium butternut squash, peeled, seeded and cubed
2 large shallots, thinly sliced
2 tbsp extra-virgin olive oil
4–6 fresh sage leaves, roughly chopped
100g (4oz) firm goat's cheese, crumbled
50g (2oz) pine nuts, toasted
350g (12oz) farfalle pasta
salt and freshly ground black pepper

1 Preheat the oven to 200°C/fan oven 180°C/Gas Mark 6. Toss the squash and shallot in the olive oil, chopped sage and seasoning. Place in a roasting tin in a single layer and roast for 30–35 minutes until tender and slightly charred, stirring occasionally. Remove from the oven, add the goat's cheese and pine kernels to the tin and toss to coat in the cooking juices.

2 While the vegetables are cooking, bring a large pan of water to the boil. Add the farfalle and cook for 10–12 minutes (or according to pack instructions) until just tender. Drain and toss with the roasted vegetables.

*Busy mum's lifesaver* Buy ready-toasted pine nuts and packs of cubed butternut squash if you're in a real hurry. You'll notice the difference in price, though!

# Roasted pepper and Italian sausage pasta

This dish is simple, convenient and quick – and really worth peeling the peppers for. When I can, I buy Italian sausages with fennel (*salsiccia finocchio*) or Luganega pork sausages from the local deli, as they are denser and more meaty than our traditional banger, but the recipe works with any good sausage. Some supermarkets do an Italian-style version with herbs, which I use in an emergency. This is in my family's top five dishes ever, known and requested simply as 'sausage pasta'. It's one of those dishes the children all clamour for when they get back from university/school/holiday and trips away.

---

*Serves 4*
*Prepare 20 minutes*
*Cook 25 minutes*

3 large peppers – red, yellow or
    orange, or a combination
450g (1lb) Italian sausages
1 tbsp olive oil
1 small onion, finely chopped
400g can chopped Italian tomatoes
350g (12oz) penne pasta
salt and freshly ground black pepper
snipped fresh basil, to garnish
freshly grated Parmesan, to serve

1 Cut the peppers into quarters, remove the seeds and carefully remove the skin, trying not to remove too much flesh – easier with a swivel vegetable peeler. Cut into 2.5cm (1in) pieces. Cut the sausages into thick slices.

2 Heat the oil in a large pan and add the onion and peppers. Cook over a medium heat for 5 minutes until softened. Add the sausages and brown on all sides. Add the tomatoes. Season and simmer for 15 minutes until the sausages are cooked through and the sauce is thickened.

3 Meanwhile cook the penne for 10–12 minutes (or according to pack instructions) and drain thoroughly. Stir a few tablespoons of snipped fresh basil into the sauce and toss with the pasta. Serve with freshly grated Parmesan.

# Singapore noodles with spicy peanut butter sauce

Peanut butter makes a great flavouring for this fast noodle dish. It's also a good way to persuade young children to eat sprouting seeds such as bean sprouts, which are packed with vitamins. The dish is traditionally made with rice noodles but I tend to use egg noodles as I'm more likely to have them in my cupboard – but you can use either.

*Serves 2–3*
*Prepare 10 minutes*
*Cook 20 minutes*

3 tbsp soy sauce
1 tbsp sesame oil (optional)
175g (6oz) pork fillet, cut into strips
300g (10oz) medium egg noodles
1 tbsp groundnut oil
2 tbsp crunchy peanut butter
2 cloves garlic, crushed
2.5cm (1in) piece fresh ginger, peeled and grated
bunch salad onions, finely sliced
1 red pepper, seeded and sliced
2 tsp medium curry powder
230g (8oz) bean sprouts or any sprouting seeds mix

1 Pour a tablespoon of soy and the sesame oil (if using) over the pork and leave to marinate for 10 minutes. Meanwhile, cook the noodles following the packet instructions and drain. Heat half the groundnut oil in a large frying pan or wok and fry the pork for 3 minutes until it is browned and just cooked through. Remove and set aside.

2 Mix the remaining soy sauce with the peanut butter. Add the remaining oil to the pan and fry the garlic and ginger for a minute until light brown. Add the salad onions and pepper and cook for 2–3 minutes until almost tender, then add the curry powder and cook for a minute. Add the bean sprouts and noodles and cooked pork with any juices and toss everything together. Add the peanut butter mix and cook, stirring, for 1 minute until heated through. Serve.

*Busy mum's lifesaver* To increase the meat/fish content add prawns or pancetta cubes with the pork and fry together. For a vegetarian version leave out the pork. Ready-to-use noodles are now available in chiller cabinets for an even speedier supper.

# Tagliatelle with caramelised onion, cauliflower and pine nuts

I've never been a huge fan of cauliflower until recently. This dish partners the veg with Middle Eastern sweet and sour flavours that seem to go down well with children and it's a real revelation – try it and you will see what I mean.

*Serves 4*
*Prepare 15 minutes*
*Cook 16 minutes*

1 tbsp olive oil
3 medium onions, thinly sliced
1 tbsp caster sugar
1 tbsp balsamic vinegar
50g (2oz) pine nuts
1 large cauliflower, broken into florets
400g (14oz) tagliatelle
chopped flat-leaf parsley
salt and freshly ground black pepper

1 Heat the oil in a frying pan, add the onions and cook over a very gentle heat for 15 minutes until really soft and golden, stirring regularly. Stir in the sugar, vinegar and pine nuts and cook for a minute longer.

2 While the onions are cooking, cook the cauliflower in a pan of boiling salted water for 3–4 minutes until just tender. Drain thoroughly and refresh under cold water. Cook the pasta for 8–10 minutes until tender. Drain.

3 Add the cauliflower to the onions. Heat through and season. Toss with the drained pasta and parsley. Check seasoning and serve.

*Busy mum's lifesaver* Cauliflower can be a bit of a handful to cut up; buy really good-quality frozen florets if you're in a hurry. Add a chopped fresh red chilli while you are cooking the onions for a more fiery flavour.

# Pea and pancetta carbonara

Adding peas to this classic dish turns it into an all-in-one meal. Since keeping my own hens carbonara has become even more of a favourite – it's great made with good free-range eggs too.

*Serves 4*
*Prepare 5 minutes*
*Cook 12 minutes*

2 medium free-range eggs
4–6 tbsp freshly grated Parmesan
400g (14oz) spaghetti
100g (4oz) frozen petits pois
100g (4oz) cubed pancetta
1 clove garlic, finely chopped
6 tbsp dry white wine
salt and freshly ground black pepper

1 Whisk together the eggs, Parmesan and seasoning in a small bowl and set aside. Cook the pasta in boiling water for 8–10 minutes until tender. Meanwhile cook the peas in boiling water for 2 minutes until just tender. Drain.

2 While the pasta is cooking, heat the pancetta in a small frying pan for a minute until the fat runs, then add the garlic. Cook for 2–3 minutes until the pancetta is crisp and golden, then add the wine and simmer for a minute or two until reduced by half. Keep the mixture warm.

3 Drain the pasta, return it to the pan and add the contents of the frying pan, the peas and the egg mixture. Return to the heat for 30 seconds and toss thoroughly together – the sauce should be creamy but don't overcook or the egg will scramble. Serve at once.

*Busy mum's lifesaver* Instead of peas try little courgettes, cubed and fried with the pancetta, or frozen sweetcorn, small broad beans or French beans cut into lengths – or a mix of all of them.

# Sausage and mushroom pappardelle

This recipe is a real taste of the winter for me – it's a cosy kind of dish for a cold night. Use a high-meat content sausage to give the right texture and flavour and to avoid the dish being too greasy. I find venison sausages work well for a change. For vegetarians simply leave out the sausages.

Serves 4
*Prepare 10 minutes*
*Cook 25 minutes*

2 tbsp olive oil
1 small onion, chopped
1 carrot, diced
1 stick celery, diced
230g (8oz) chestnut mushrooms, sliced
500g (1lb 2oz) good-quality sausages, sliced thickly
100ml (4fl oz) red wine
200g can chopped Italian tomatoes
2 sprigs fresh rosemary
350g (12oz) pappardelle pasta
salt and freshly ground black pepper
freshly grated Parmesan, to serve

1 Heat the oil in a sauté pan and fry the onion, carrot and celery together for 3 minutes until softened. Add the mushrooms and cook for a further 3–4 minutes until browned, then add the sausages and brown them quickly over a high heat.

2 Add the wine, tomatoes, rosemary and seasoning to the pan and simmer, covered, for 15 minutes until the sausages are cooked through. Check seasoning. While the sauce is cooking, cook the pappardelle for 8–10 minutes (or according to pack instructions) in a large pan of boiling water until just tender. Drain the pasta and toss with the sauce. Serve with freshly grated Parmesan.

*Busy mum's lifesaver* The quality of the sausages makes all the difference with this dish. Make double quantities and freeze half for emergencies.

# fall-back favourites

These dishes are the ones I make when I get in from work feeling totally exhausted – the planning has gone out of the window, the shops are closed and I've forgotten to place an online order. I can turn to one of these knowing everyone, including me, will be happy. All the ingredients will be somewhere in the kitchen and if not I can substitute something else – thank heaven for the freezer, the microwave and the wonders of the canning process. ⟶

# Bottom-drawer minestrone

A really well-flavoured minestrone makes a good fast supper or Saturday lunch all year round, and is great for using up the bits and bobs of veg that may lurk in the fridge. Use a range of veg depending on what you can find – I've listed some typical ingredients. Make up a big batch of soup; it will keep in the fridge for a couple of days – you could even take a flask to work.

⟶ Serve with warm ciabatta.

*Serves 3–4*
*Prepare 15 minutes*
*Cook 40 minutes*

1 tbsp olive oil
1 large onion, finely chopped
1 clove garlic, crushed
75g (3oz) cubed pancetta (optional)
2 carrots, peeled and diced
2 sticks celery, diced
400g can Italian plum tomatoes
1 courgette, diced
½ cabbage/kale/greens, shredded
400g can cannellini beans, drained
1 litre (1¾ pint) vegetable or
   chicken stock (see page 28)
salt and freshly ground black pepper
freshly grated Parmesan, to serve
extra-virgin olive oil, to serve

1 Heat the oil in a pan and add the onion, garlic, pancetta, carrots and celery and cook over a low heat for 10 minutes until soft but not browned. Add the tomatoes and courgette and simmer for a further 15 minutes.

2 Stir in the cabbage and beans and the stock. Season and bring to the boil. Simmer for 10–15 minutes until the vegetables are tender. Check seasoning and serve in warm deep soup bowls with a drizzle of extra-virgin olive oil and freshly grated Parmesan.

*Busy mum's lifesaver* Try adding a teaspoon of pesto to each serving. For a richer version replace 150ml (¼ pint) of the stock with red wine and add 50–100g (2–4oz) small pasta shapes or soup pasta if you have it.

# Spanish chicken with chorizo

A real family favourite at any time of the year. Whole chicken thighs with skin and bone give the best flavour, but you can use any chicken joints. Try Romano peppers for their sweet flavour, but if you're in a hurry, substitute a jar of ready-grilled peppers.

→ Serve with baked potatoes and broccoli in winter; with bread and a salad in summer.

*Serves 4*
*Prepare 20 minutes*
*Cook 1¼ hours*

8 large free-range chicken thighs
2 tbsp olive oil
250g (9oz) mini cooking chorizo, cubed
1 medium onion, finely chopped
2 cloves garlic, chopped
3 red and yellow peppers, seeded and thinly sliced
200g can chopped Italian tomatoes
2 fresh bay leaves
150ml (¼ pint) dry white wine
salt and freshly ground black pepper
chopped parsley, to garnish

1 Preheat the oven to 190°C/fan oven 170°C/Gas Mark 5. Season the chicken pieces. Heat the oil in a large flameproof casserole and cook the chicken thighs on a high heat on all sides until golden brown. Do this in two batches. Drain on kitchen paper.

2 Add the chorizo to the pan and cook for a minute, then add the onion, garlic and peppers. Stir over a medium heat for 5 minutes until starting to brown then add the tomatoes, bay leaves, wine and seasoning to the pan. Return the chicken pieces to the pan and bring to the boil. Cover the pan and transfer to the oven for an hour until the chicken is completely cooked through. Garnish with parsley and serve.

*Busy mum's lifesaver* Mini cooking chorizo is now available in the supermarket or good delis and really makes a difference to the end result of this dish. Use cubed pancetta or sliced regular chorizo in an emergency.

# Chicken, thyme and potato bake

This all-in-one dish really couldn't be more simple – get back from work, put all the ingredients together in a roasting tin and shove it in the oven for an hour and then sit down to eat. It's also a good way to cook sausages or pork chops.

→ Serve with shredded kale or cabbage.

-----

*Serves 4*
*Prepare 15 minutes*
*Cook 1 hour*

1 tbsp olive oil
650g (1¼lb) new potatoes, scrubbed and thickly sliced
3 tbsp onion marmalade
2 eating apples, peeled, cored and thickly sliced
2 tbsp chopped fresh thyme
8 free-range chicken thighs
450ml (¾ pint) chicken stock (see page 28)
salt and freshly ground black pepper

1 Preheat the oven to 180°C/fan oven 160°C/ Gas Mark 4. Heat the oil in a large heavy-duty roasting tin on the hob, add the potatoes and cook over a high heat for 2–3 minutes until starting to brown. Remove from the heat and stir through the onion marmalade.

2 Add the apples to the tin and toss with the thyme and plenty of seasoning. Tuck the chicken thighs amongst the potatoes and apples in a single layer then pour over the chicken stock to almost cover. Bake for 50–55 minutes until the potatoes are tender and the chicken is golden and cooked through.

*Busy mum's lifesaver* Look out for jars of onion marmalade or caramelised onions on the same shelf as the chutneys in many food shops. A spoonful or two adds flavour to all kinds of stews and cheesy dishes, too.

# Salmon and ginger pastry parcels

Frozen puff pastry made with butter is the key to these little parcels. Making pastry is out of the question – far too much labour for the end result. The vegetable-fat readymade versions available until recently were a little disappointing when it came to flavour. Not so with the new butter varieties. Make up the parcels and leave them in the fridge – then cook to order as needed on those occasions when everyone arrives back home at different times.

→ Serve with boiled new potatoes and a green vegetable or salad.

*Serves 4*
*Prepare 20 minutes*
*Cook 20 minutes*

50g (2oz) butter, at room temperature
2.5cm (1in) piece fresh ginger, peeled
  and finely chopped
2 tbsp chopped flat-leaf parsley
1 tbsp lemon juice
375g block puff pastry made
  with butter, thawed if frozen
4 skinless salmon fillets, weighing
  about 100g (4oz) each
beaten egg, to glaze
salt and freshly ground black pepper

1 Preheat the oven to 200°C/fan oven 180°C/Gas Mark 6. Beat the butter with the ginger, parsley, lemon juice and seasoning. Roll out the pastry to about 5mm (¼in) thick and cut into four squares that will completely cover the fish fillets.

2 Place a salmon fillet in the centre of each pastry square and spread a quarter of the flavoured butter on top of each fillet. Brush the edges of the pastry with cold water and wrap the pastry over the fish, pressing to seal the edges. Place the parcels on a dampened baking sheet, sealed side down. Chill until needed.

3 Mark a diamond pattern on the pastry with the blade of a knife. Brush the parcels with beaten egg and bake for 18–20 minutes until the pastry is puffy and golden.

*Busy mum's lifesaver* Use any kind of pastry, whatever's in the freezer or fridge – try butter shortcrust or filo. NB Don't defrost pastry in the microwave, it turns into a gooey mess.

# Spiced chickpeas with spinach

Spinach makes the perfect quick supper dish, used here with canned chickpeas. I have started growing spinach in my new raised vegetable beds but frozen is a great alternative – or use the tender bagged variety from the supermarket.

→ Serve with basmati rice or warmed naan bread and a yogurt raita.

*Serves 3–4*
*Prepare 15 minutes*
*Cook 25 minutes*

2 tbsp sunflower oil
1 large onion, chopped
2 cloves garlic, finely chopped
2 tsp grated fresh root ginger
1 tbsp ground coriander
2 tsp ground cumin
1 tsp ground turmeric
½ tsp dried chilli flakes
400g can chopped Italian tomatoes
2 x 400g cans chickpeas, including
   canning liquid
salt
1 tsp garam masala
450g (1lb) fresh spinach, washed and
   leaves shredded, or 230g (8oz)
   frozen leaf spinach

1 Heat the oil in a large saucepan, add the onion, garlic and ginger and fry gently for 5 minutes until soft and lightly browned. Stir in the coriander, cumin, turmeric and chilli and cook for a further minute then stir in the tomatoes and their juices and bring to a gentle boil. Simmer, stirring occasionally, for 5 minutes to give a thick sauce.

2 Add the chickpeas and their liquid, salt and garam masala and bring back to simmering point. Cover and cook gently for 10 minutes. (You can prepare the dish to this stage and leave to cool then finish just before you need it.)

3 Stir in the spinach then turn up the heat and cook for 5 minutes until the spinach is tender and the liquid has almost evaporated. Check the seasoning and serve.

*Busy mum's lifesaver* Use 1 tbsp good-quality medium curry powder instead of the individual spices. For a quick yogurt raita, stir chopped mint and grated cucumber into natural yogurt and flavour with lemon juice, a pinch of chilli powder, salt and pepper.

# Smoked haddock, pea and leek chowder

If you have a good fishmonger, buy the best fish you can and you will see the difference in flavour when you make this hearty soup. I get mine from Paul 'The Fish' at my local farmers' market – the catch comes straight up from Hastings and the smoke is a subtle yet satisfying one. The dish is another regular favourite as the whole family love smoked haddock.

⟶ Serve with crusty bread.

*Serves 4*
*Prepare 15 minutes*
*Cook 35 minutes*

a walnut-sized knob of butter
3 medium leeks, thinly sliced
500g (1lb 2oz) floury potatoes, such as
  King Edward, peeled and diced
1 litre (1¾ pint) semi-skimmed milk
400g (14oz) smoked haddock fillet,
  cut into cubes
230g (8oz) frozen peas
3 tbsp snipped chives
salt and freshly ground black pepper

1 Heat the butter in a large pan and add the leeks. Cook over a low heat for 6–7 minutes until really soft but not browned. Add the diced potato and stir for a couple of minutes then pour in the milk and bring to the boil. Simmer for 12–15 minutes until the vegetables are almost cooked through.

2 Add the cubed smoked haddock and peas to the pan and simmer gently for 5 minutes until the fish is just cooked through. Stir in the chives and season to taste. Serve in warmed bowls.

*Busy mum's lifesaver* Look out for good-quality frozen chopped herbs in sachets at the supermarket. Use frozen fish fillets in an emergency – the dish will work just as well.

# Corned beef, red onion and sweet potato hash

Try this dish when you've got nothing left in the fridge. My version uses sweet potato for a change, but leftover cooked potato works perfectly. It's cheap, filling and comforting – perfect family food. I associate this dish with winter evenings when we get back in the dark from sporty events and everyone is 'starving'. Some members of the family have to have it with tomato ketchup, which I abominate with anything except chips (although it does have its uses as a cooking ingredient).

⟶ Serve with steamed broccoli.

*Serves 4*
*Prepare 15 minutes*
*Cook 30 minutes*

650g (1¼lb) sweet potatoes,
   scrubbed and cut into large chunks
150g (5oz) frozen peas
1 large red onion, finely chopped
340g can corned beef, cubed
4–6 tbsp chopped flat-leaf parsley
1–2 tbsp chilli sauce
2 tbsp olive oil
salt and freshly ground black pepper

1 Cook the sweet potatoes in a large pan of boiling water for 12–15 minutes until just tender. Drain and, when cool enough to handle, cut into 2.5cm (1in) cubes. Cook the peas in boiling water for 2 minutes and drain.

2 Mix the cubed potato, peas, onion, corned beef, parsley, chilli sauce and seasoning together in a mixing bowl. Heat the oil in a large non-stick frying pan, add the corned beef mixture and cook, stirring, over a medium heat until the mixture starts to brown and the potatoes crispen up.

3 Preheat the grill. Pat the hash mixture to level the surface, and turn up the heat under the pan to brown the base for a couple of minutes. Then place the pan under the grill for 3–4 minutes to brown the top. Cut into wedges to serve.

*Busy mum's lifesaver* **Try serving with a fried egg on top for an even more substantial supper.**

# Squash and pancetta risotto

Risotto is one of the most versatile store-cupboard dishes as there are so many variations. In summer I make pea, courgette and broad bean; in the darker months this one is made with colourful squash or pumpkin – a good way to use up all the flesh leftover from pumpkin lanterns at Halloween. The original inspiration came from a wonderful book by Valentina Harris, *Risotto! Risotto!* – now sadly out of print but worth hunting for on the internet.

⟶ Serve with a leafy green salad.

*Serves 4*
*Prepare 15 minutes*
*Cook 40 minutes*

1 tbsp olive oil
1 medium onion, finely chopped
75g (3oz) cubed pancetta
1 medium butternut squash, peeled, seeded and cubed
1 litre (1¾ pints) chicken stock (see page 28)
1 tbsp chopped fresh sage
250g (9oz) risotto rice
75ml (3floz) dry white wine
3 tbsp grated Parmesan cheese
25g (1oz) butter
salt and freshly ground black pepper

1 Put the oil, onion and pancetta in a medium non-stick pan. Cook over a medium heat for 2–3 minutes until softened. Add the cubed squash and cook over a medium heat for 12–15 minutes until the squash is tender and golden brown. While the squash is cooking, pour the chicken stock into a separate pan and bring it to a simmer.

2 Stir the sage and rice into the cooked squash and cook for a minute to coat in the pan juices, then stir in the white wine.

3 Gradually add the hot stock to the rice, a ladleful at a time. Keep stirring: the mixture should bubble gently until each ladleful of stock is absorbed. Then add the next ladleful and carry on stirring. The whole process will take 15–20 minutes, by which time you should have a creamy risotto with the rice just tender but not mushy.

4 Off the heat stir in the Parmesan and butter. Check seasoning and serve the risotto in warmed bowls.

# Pesto and pepper pork

This is one of the simplest and best recipes I've ever written. It's just so easy and quick and completely delicious. I came up with it for a work project recently and although it has appeared elsewhere, I had to include it for anyone who missed it. Use any type of leftover pesto but basil is particularly good.
→ Serve with a salad and bread to mop up the juices.

*Serves 4*
*Prepare 10 minutes*
*Cook 25 minutes*

1 tbsp olive oil
4 large free-range pork chops
2 red, yellow or orange peppers, seeded and sliced lengthways
3 large vine tomatoes, roughly chopped
150ml (¼ pint) dry white wine
4 tbsp pesto
salt and freshly ground black pepper

1 Heat the oil in a sauté pan or large non-stick frying pan and brown the chops on both sides for 3–4 minutes. Remove and keep warm. Add the sliced peppers to the pan and cook for 5 minutes until soft and browned, then add the tomatoes and cook for a further couple of minutes until pulpy. Return the chops to the pan.

2 Pour over the wine and bring to the boil. Season then cover the pan and simmer for 8–10 minutes until the chops are cooked through and the juices run clear when pierced. Stir the pesto into the peppers and juices in the pan.

# Crispy bacon and egg salad

An easy salad that can be made at any time of the year. I make it for myself, as it contains all my favourite bits and pieces – and it's simple to up the ingredients if I'm cooking for more. In the summer I use salad grown in pots outside the kitchen door. The better quality the bread for the croutons, the better the finished result.

*Per person*
*Prepare 10 minutes*
*Cook 10 minutes*

50g (2oz) cubed pancetta
4 tsp extra-virgin olive oil
1 slice day-old (or older) sour dough
   or ciabatta bread, cubed
50g (2oz) baby leaf salad or rocket
   salad
3–4 cherry tomatoes on the vine,
   quartered
½ avocado, sliced
½ small red onion, thinly sliced
1 tsp balsamic vinegar
1 tsp white wine vinegar
1 large free-range egg
salt and freshly ground black pepper

1 Dry-fry the pancetta for 3–4 minutes in a heavy-based frying pan until crisp and golden. Drain on kitchen paper. Add 1 tsp of the oil to the pan and fry the bread cubes over a medium heat until golden and crisp. Drain on kitchen paper.

2 Pile the salad leaves into the base of a serving dish. Scatter over the tomatoes, avocado, onion, pancetta and croutons. Whisk together the rest of the oil and the balsamic vinegar with seasoning and drizzle over the salad.

3 Crack the egg into a cup. Heat a pan of water and add the white wine vinegar. Slide in the egg and simmer very gently for 3 minutes until just set. Remove from the pan with a slotted spoon and place gently on top of the salad. Season the egg and serve.

*Busy mum's lifesaver* Replace the pancetta with 25g (1oz) toasted pine nuts for vegetarians.

# Warm potato, tuna and tomato salad

A really easy salad that makes a perfect quick summer supper or lunch.
→ Serve with crusty ciabatta bread to mop up any leftover dressing.

*Serves 3–4*
*Prepare 10 minutes*
*Cook 15 minutes*

500g (1lb 2oz) small to medium new
   potatoes, scrubbed
4 large free-range eggs
3 tbsp extra-virgin olive oil
1 tbsp red wine vinegar
1 tsp capers, chopped
200g can tuna in olive oil, drained and
   broken into chunks
230g (8oz) cherry plum tomatoes,
   halved
1 small red onion, finely sliced
salt and freshly ground black pepper

1 Cook the potatoes in a pan of simmering water for 15 minutes until just tender; drain and cut into chunks. Meanwhile, place the eggs in a pan of cold water, bring to the boil and simmer for 8 minutes. Run them under cold water to cool; peel and cut into wedges. Whisk the oil and vinegar with the capers and seasoning. Place the warm potatoes in a salad bowl and pour over the dressing. Toss gently.

2 Add the remaining ingredients to the warm potato and turn over with a spoon to coat in the dressing.

*Busy mum's lifesaver* Use the oil from the tuna can for the dressing. Try drained canned cannellini beans instead of potatoes for a change, and add a handful of chopped fresh basil or flat-leaf parsley if you have some.

# weekend wonders

When my children were small I worked with a lovely food magazine editor who used to spend the weekend making her own squid-ink pasta and other wonderful foodie treats. She didn't have children! At that time I seemed to spend most of my weekend in the car – either on the way to the supermarket or picking the girls up from ballet or stuck in traffic ferrying small (noisy!) children to a party. I dreamed of the day when I could return to such culinary activities. Sadly, I've learned you can never go back – even now the children are older, the moment seems to have passed. I do get enormous pleasure from cooking but there is so much else to do I tend to keep it fairly simple – if I want more sophisticated dining, I eat out. But I do enjoy having the time to cook more time-consuming dishes. And weekends can be a good opportunity to rope the children in to help out. The dishes here take longer to prepare/need a bit of time to cook/or improve with keeping, and for those reasons get relegated to weekend cooking sessions. Many are great for having in the fridge or freezer for the week ahead and, of course, I've included a couple of good roasts for Sunday gatherings. →

# Spiced roasted belly pork with caramelised sweet potatoes

Despite its trendy image as the chefs' favourite, belly pork is a well-priced choice for feeding the family. Cooking it long and slow allows the fat and meat to melt into silky shreds and the skin to turn into crisp yet tender crackling – delicious!

→ Serve with a selection of vegetables.

*Serves 6–8*
*Prepare 10 minutes plus 2 hours*
*marinating time*
*Cook 3–3½ hours*

2kg (4lb) piece belly pork
2 tsp five-spice powder
1 tsp freshly ground black pepper
3 tbsp thick honey
1 tbsp coarse sea salt
750g (1¾lb) sweet potatoes, scrubbed
and cut into wedges

1 Pierce the skin of the pork all over with a skewer then pour boiling water over it. Pat dry with kitchen paper. Mix together the five-spice powder, pepper, half the honey and salt and rub all over the underside of the pork. Leave to marinate for at least 2 hours.

2 Preheat the oven to 200°C/fan oven 180°C/ Gas Mark 6. Place the pork skin side up on a rack set over a roasting tin. Roast for 30 minutes. Lower the temperature to 170°C/fan oven 150°C/ Gas Mark 3. Cook the pork for a further 2–2½ hours until the skin is tender and starting to crisp.

3 Cook the sweet potatoes in boiling water for 5 minutes and drain. Remove the pork from the oven, pour off any fat and remove the rack. Return the pork to the tin and add the potatoes around it. Toss in the juices and sprinkle with the remaining honey, and then return to a really hot oven at 230°C/fan oven 210°C/ Gas Mark 8 for a further 20–30 minutes until the potatoes are crisp and golden and the crackling is crisp.

4 Remove the pork from the oven, place on a serving dish and leave to rest for 5 minutes. Slice and serve with any pan juices and the roasted sweet potatoes.

*Busy mum's lifesaver* Ask for the bones to be removed if buying belly pork from traditional butchers. Try slicing the cold pork very thinly for sandwiches – delicious with mango chutney and salad or mayonnaise and tomato.

# Family choice pizzas

If you've never attempted to make bread, pizza is a great place to start. It's so easy to make with easy-blend yeast. I often make a double batch of dough and use half for pizza and then make a loaf of focaccia with the rest and freeze it for later (it's great for picnics). If you have a bread maker, by all means use it, but I enjoy the occasional kneading session – it gets rid of some of the week's frustrations! Then let everyone enjoy adding his or her own topping.

→ Serve with a big bowl of leafy salad.

*Makes 4 pizzas*
*Prepare 25 minutes*
*Proving 1–1½ hours*
*Cook 20 minutes*

500g (1lb 2oz) Italian 00 flour or
    strong white bread flour
1½ tsp salt
2 tsp easy-blend yeast
2 tbsp olive oil
1 amount tomato sauce (see page 40)
toppings, see step 3

1 Sift the flour and salt into a mixing bowl and stir in the yeast. Whisk the oil with 300ml (½ pint) warm water and add to the flour. Mix to a soft dough and turn on to a lightly floured work surface. Knead for 10 minutes until smooth and elastic. Place in a clean oiled bowl and cover with oiled cling wrap. Leave in a warm corner of the kitchen for 45 minutes or until doubled in size.

2 Preheat the oven to 220°C/fan oven 200°C/Gas Mark 7. Turn the dough out on to a floured surface and knead lightly to knock out any air. Divide into four and roll out to really thin circles about 2cm (¾in) thick. Transfer to floured baking sheets. Spread the tomato sauce over the middle, leaving a border.

3 Scatter with your chosen topping. For a classic Margherita add torn pieces of buffalo mozzarella, shredded fresh basil and a drizzle of extra-virgin olive oil. Or try crumbled goat's cheese, thinly sliced red onion and basil pesto; or cooked red peppers, cubed cooking chorizo and an egg broken into the centre. Or add this combo to the baked pizza: fresh rocket, Parma ham and Parmesan shavings.

4 Cover with cling wrap and leave to prove for 15 minutes until puffy. Bake in the oven for 15–20 minutes until the top is golden and bubbling and the dough crisp.

*Busy mum's lifesaver* Bake rosemary focaccia at the same time. Roll out the dough to a rectangle about 25–30cm (10–12in), cover with cling wrap and leave to prove for 20 minutes until puffy. Make dents all over the surface with your thumbs and simply scatter with snipped fresh rosemary, drizzle with oil and scatter with sea salt. Bake for 25 minutes until golden.

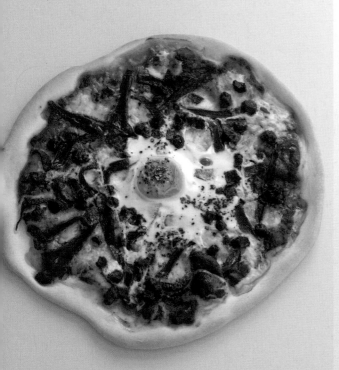

# Lamb and cumin stew with roasted aubergine

Tomatoey, spicy and warming, this dish warrants an overused term: it's a true winter warmer. If you cook it and leave it for a day or two, it tastes even better as the flavours intensify and meld together. I make it at the weekend and keep it in the fridge for a delicious midweek supper.
→ Serve with noodles or bread to mop up the juices.

------

*Serves 4–6*
*Prepare 20 minutes*
*Cook 2 hours*

1 large aubergine, thickly sliced
2 tbsp olive oil
650g (1¼lb) cubed shoulder of lamb/ stewing lamb
1 large onion, thinly sliced
2 cloves garlic, finely chopped
2 tsp ground cumin
400g can chopped Italian tomatoes
juice of ½ lemon
200ml (7floz) soured cream
3 tbsp chopped fresh mint
salt and freshly ground black pepper

1 Preheat the oven to 200°C/fan oven180°C/ Gas Mark 6. Place the aubergine slices in a small roasting tin in a single layer and drizzle with half the oil. Season then roast in the oven for 45–50 minutes until charred and golden.

2 Meanwhile heat the remaining oil in a flameproof casserole and brown the lamb well on all sides. Remove with a slotted spoon. Add the onion and garlic to the casserole and cook for 5 minutes until soft and golden. Stir in the cumin and cook for a minute.

3 Return the lamb to the pan with any juices and add the tomatoes, lemon juice and seasoning. Add about 150ml (¼ pint) water, bring to the boil, then cover and place in the oven for 45 minutes.

4 Cut the roast aubergine slices in half then stir into the lamb. Return the casserole to the oven and cook, uncovered, for a further 15–20 minutes until the lamb is tender and cooked through. Stir the soured cream and chopped mint together then stir into the lamb but don't mix in completely – you want a marbled effect. Check the seasoning and serve.

# Crispy duck with Sarladaise potatoes

On a family holiday near Sarlat in the south-west of France we all fell for the local duck and goose dishes served with potatoes cooked in the birds' fat with lots of garlic and parsley. This is my version to cook at home. It's a dish that epitomises the French paradox – people from the area eat dishes cooked in duck fat but it seems to promote good health! The potatoes can be served with a fried egg or two on top or with pork or lamb instead. But they're best of all with crisp confit of duck. Buy confit in large cans or vacuum packed at the supermarket (or bring it back from trips to France).

➡ Serve with steamed kale or cabbage.

*Serves 4*
*Prepare 10 minutes plus 30 minutes
    waiting*
*Cook 25 minutes*

4 confit duck legs with their fat
4 medium floury potatoes, such as
    King Edward, peeled and really
    thinly sliced
2 cloves garlic, chopped
4 tbsp chopped flat-leaf parsley
3 tbsp duck fat (from the confit or use
    goose fat from the supermarket)
salt and freshly ground black pepper

1 Place the duck legs in a shallow roasting tin skin side up with space between them and leave for 30 minutes or so to come to room temperature. This will allow the fat to liquefy and you can pour or spoon some of it off. Toss the sliced potatoes with the garlic, chopped parsley, plenty of seasoning and 3 tablespoons of the duck fat to coat. Brush a 20cm (8in) shallow cake tin with duck fat and arrange the potato slices in circles to form a thin cake. Preheat the oven to 220°C/fan oven 200°C/Gas Mark 7.

2 Place the potatoes in the oven and cook for 10 minutes. Turn the duck skin side down and cook in the oven next to the potato cake for a further 20–25 minutes. The duck should be crisp and golden, turn it once during cooking. The potato cake should be cooked through and golden. Serve the duck with wedges of the potato.

*Busy mum's lifesaver* Substitute regular duck breasts for the confit: arrange them on a rack over a roasting tin and cook for 20–25 minutes until the skin is crisp and they are just pink.

# Slow-cooked shoulder of lamb with rosemary cider rice

This good all-in-one pot dish makes a simple family lunch or evening meal. As a joint, shoulder of lamb is tricky to carve and serve. However, now it's more readily available boned and rolled, making it far easier to deal with and well worth trying for its wonderful flavour and succulent meat.

→ Serve with steamed broccoli.

*Serves 4–6*
*Prepare 10 minutes*
*Cook 1¾ hours*

1kg (2¼lb) boned, rolled shoulder of
   lamb joint
1 tsp smoked paprika
2 tbsp olive oil
2 sprigs fresh rosemary
2 cloves garlic
230g (8oz) risotto or paella rice
200ml (7floz) dry cider or dry white
   wine
200ml (7floz) vegetable or chicken
   stock (see page 28)
salt and freshly ground black pepper

1 Preheat the oven to 170°C/fan oven 150°C/ Gas Mark 3. Rub the lamb skin with the paprika, salt and pepper. Heat the oil in a flameproof casserole and brown the lamb really well on all sides. Add the rosemary and garlic to the pan then cover and cook in the oven for 1 hour.

2 Remove the casserole from the oven and stir the rice into the juices around the lamb. Stir in the cider, stock and seasoning. Raise the temperature to 180°C/fan oven160°C/ Gas Mark 4 and cook for a further 35–45 minutes uncovered, until the rice is tender and all the liquid absorbed. Stir the rice halfway through cooking.

3 Remove from the oven and leave the lamb to rest for 5–10 minutes before carving. Serve with the rice.

# Chicken and ham parsley pie

A really good chicken pie makes a change from roast on a Sunday and is a good choice after a heavy Saturday night! Most of the preparation and cooking can be done the day before, which means you can have a lie-in – and there is far less washing-up on the day.

➡ Serve with lots of creamy mash and peas or runner beans when in season.

-----------------------------------

*Serves 6*
*Prepare 20 minutes*
*Cook 2 hours*

1 good-quality free-range chicken, about 1.5 kg (3¼lb)
stock vegetables: a carrot, onion, celery stick, leek, all cut into chunks
stock herbs: 1 bay leaf, 6 peppercorns, sprig or two of fresh thyme
50g (2oz) butter
1 medium onion, chopped
50g (2oz) plain flour
50ml (2floz) double cream
4 tbsp chopped flat-leaf parsley
150g (5oz) good-quality sliced ham, chopped
375g pack puff pastry made with butter, thawed if frozen
beaten egg, to glaze
salt and freshly ground black pepper

1 Place the chicken in a large pan that fits it neatly with the stock vegetables and herbs. Pour over enough cold water to almost cover and a large pinch of salt. Bring to the boil and then cover and simmer very gently for 45–50 minutes until the chicken juices run clear when the thickest part of the leg is pierced with a skewer. Cool in the stock for a really good moist finish. Strain the stock and measure out 600ml (1 pint). Freeze the remainder for soups etc.

2 Preheat the oven to 200°C/fan oven 180°C/Gas Mark 6. Melt the butter in a large non-stick pan and add the onion. Cook gently for 3–4 minutes until soft and pale. Add the flour and stir for a minute to cook. Off the heat gradually whisk in the hot stock then return to the heat and simmer, stirring until thick and smooth. Stir in the cream, parsley and seasoning.

3 Remove the chicken meat from the bones, discarding the skin. Tear into pieces and mix with the ham in the base of a 1.75 litre (3 pint) ovenproof dish or roasting tin with a wide lip to hold the pastry. Pour over the sauce (you can make the pie to this stage then cool and chill overnight).

4 Place a ceramic eggcup or funnel in the centre of the dish to support the pastry. Roll out the pastry on a lightly floured work surface to a rectangle 5cm (2in) larger than the dish. Cut a strip about 1.5cm (½in) wide and place along the edge of the pie dish. Brush the pastry edge on the dish with cold water then lift the rectangle of pastry over and settle it gently on the filling. Pinch around the edges to seal and make a hole in the centre to allow steam to escape. Chill for 15 minutes to allow the pastry to rest then brush with beaten egg and bake for 45–50 minutes until the pie is crisp and golden.

# Meatball, pesto and mozzarella lasagne

This is another great dish to pack if you are driving a long way to a self-catering destination (see also roast honey and cumin chicken page 26). Prepare and assemble it in a sturdy dish (I use a deep roasting tin) or foil container, chill and wrap securely, then pack it in a cold bag and put in the car where you can find it easily when you arrive. Don't expect the usual very saucy lasagne as you assemble it. It may seem dry but the end result is marvellous.

→ Serve with a rocket and vine tomato salad.

*Serves 4*
*Prepare 30 minutes*
*Cook 55 minutes*

230g (8oz) each minced beef and pork
1 medium free-range egg, beaten
3 tbsp dried white breadcrumbs
25g (1oz) grated Parmesan
1 tbsp olive oil
150g (5oz) good-quality roasted
    pepper pesto
300g (10oz) fresh lasagne sheets
230g (8oz) mozzarella, sliced
½ amount béchamel sauce (see
    page 34)
salt and freshly ground black pepper

1 Preheat the oven to 190°C/fan oven 170°C/Gas Mark 5. Mix the minced beef and pork with the egg, breadcrumbs, half the Parmesan and seasoning. Roll the mixture into small balls the size of walnuts. Heat the oil in a non-stick frying pan and cook the meatballs until golden all over and cooked through – this will take about 6–8 minutes. Drain on kitchen paper.

2 Spread a little pesto over the base of a 1.75 litre (3 pint) greased ovenproof baking dish. Cover with a layer of lasagne sheets. Top with a third each of the meatballs, mozzarella and pesto, then add another layer of lasagne sheets. Keep on layering, finishing with a layer of lasagne. Spread over the béchamel sauce and scatter with the remaining Parmesan.

3 Bake in the oven for 40–45 minutes until the pasta is tender and the top is golden.

*Busy mum's lifesaver* Use fresh lasagne if you can, as it makes it easier to assemble the dish. If you use dried lasagne, pre-cook the sheets in boiling water first.

# feed the hordes

As our children become more independent, mums everywhere agree that catering for them is one of the biggest challenges of all. Thanks to mobiles and social networking, their plans change all the time. One moment you think you are catering for a large number of 'starving' teenagers, only to be told that it's all off and they are going to some other obliging parent instead. It's all too easy to turn into a moaning harridan and put them off inviting friends round altogether. I try to find a balance: good food, maybe a bed when given adequate warning – but not an open invitation to all, with taxi service as an added extra. These are the meals I serve them if they follow the rules (and sometimes if not!) – bulky enough to fill them up but won't break the bank.

I also turn to these recipes for family gatherings such as picnics or barbecues. They are flexible enough to serve at different occasions and a key point is that many can be prepared in advance then left in the fridge – just put them in the oven when needed. A good number of them can be frozen too – make up double quantities and freeze half and you'll never be caught out when the hordes descend. ⟶

# Thai red salmon curry with green beans and lentils

Adding lentils is a good way of stretching the fish or meat element of a dish and, as this fish curry has lots of delicious sauce, you can make it go even further by serving with plenty of rice – a good trick when hit with extra numbers. If really desperate, double up the lentils and curry paste and stir in another tin of coconut milk – it still tastes good and fills everyone up satisfactorily.

→ Serve with steamed rice.

*Serves 6*
*Prepare 10 minutes*
*Cook 20 minutes*

230g (8oz) Puy lentils
1 tbsp sunflower oil
300g (10oz) French beans, topped, tailed and halved
3 yellow peppers, seeded and sliced
650g (1¼lb) salmon fillet, cubed
50–75g (2–3oz) good-quality Thai red curry paste
2 x 400g cans coconut milk
1 small red onion, sliced
shredded fresh basil, to garnish

1 Rinse the lentils, place in a medium pan and generously cover with water. Bring to the boil and simmer for 15 minutes until just tender. Drain thoroughly. While the lentils are cooking, heat the oil in a heavy-based pan and add the beans and sliced pepper. Cook for a couple of minutes then add the cubed salmon and stir together for a minute.

2 Stir the curry paste into the pan and cook for a minute to coat the salmon in the paste. Add the coconut milk, bring to the boil and simmer gently for 4–5 minutes until the salmon is just cooked through. Add the lentils then scatter with the sliced onions and basil.

*Busy mum's lifesaver* The better-quality Thai curry pastes are so good it is not worth making your own. In the winter substitute spinach, shredded cabbage or kale for the French beans.

# That cheesy potato skiing dish

A holiday favourite based on the French Savoie dish Tartiflette, this recipe is tailor-made for a large group of hungry young people. You can prepare it and leave it covered in the fridge ready for them to put in the oven. The original is made with authentic Reblochon cheese but a budget version using Brie or Camembert is almost as good.

→ Serve with a salad.

*Serves 6*
*Prepare 25 minutes*
*Cook 1 hour*

1.35kg (3lb) medium-sized waxy
  potatoes, scrubbed (and peeled if
  you have time but fine if not)
25g (1oz) butter
2 tbsp olive oil
2 medium onions, thinly sliced
2 cloves garlic, crushed
230g (8oz) smoked bacon lardons
1 Reblochon cheese
150ml (¼ pint) single cream
salt and freshly ground black pepper

1 Preheat the oven to 220°C/ fan oven 200°C/Gas Mark 7. Cover the potatoes in cold water, bring to the boil and cook for 20–25 minutes until cooked through. Drain then cool slightly and cut into 1cm (½in) slices.

2 Heat the butter and olive oil in a frying pan; add the onion and garlic and cook gently for 5 minutes. Add the bacon to the pan and cook for a further 5 minutes, until the onion and bacon are lightly coloured.

3 Cut the cheese in half across the centre horizontally, rind and all; then cut each piece horizontally again so you have four flat discs. Arrange a layer of potatoes in the base of a 2.5 litre (4 pint) buttered ovenproof dish and scatter over some of the onion and bacon. Lightly season with salt and pepper. Repeat the layers. Arrange the cheese discs on top; pour the cream over the cheese and bake for 20–25 minutes until golden and bubbling. Leave to stand for 5 minutes, for the flavours to develop.

# Roasted vegetable and goat's cheese lasagne

Made properly, a good vegetable lasagne is a great choice for feeding large numbers of teenagers of unknown food preferences. The substantial mix of carbs and fat make a proper stomach lining in advance of a heavy night of partying. You can always partner it with a meat version (see page 34) to satisfy the carnivores in the group.

→ Serve with a green salad.

*Serves 6*
*Prepare 10 minutes*
*Cook 1¼ hours*

1 large aubergine, sliced
3 red peppers, seeded and sliced
4 ripe tomatoes, halved
2 red onions, cut into wedges
2 tbsp olive oil
1 tbsp sun-dried tomato paste
230g (8oz) lasagne verde, dried
1 amount béchamel sauce (see page 34)
100g (4oz) firm goat's cheese, crumbled
4 tbsp grated Parmesan or vegetarian Cheddar
salt and freshly ground black pepper

1 Preheat the oven to 200°C/fan oven 180°C/Gas Mark 6. Place the vegetables in a roasting tin in a single layer and pour over the olive oil and seasoning. Roast for 30–35 minutes until tender and just charred. Stir in the tomato paste.

2 Spread a little of the béchamel sauce over the base of a 2.5 litre (4 pint) baking dish. Arrange a layer of lasagne over the top, then a layer of the roasted vegetables, followed by some goat's cheese. Continue layering up sauce, vegetables, cheese and pasta, finishing with a layer of pasta. Pour a thin layer of béchamel sauce on top and scatter with Parmesan.

3 Bake for 35–40 minutes until bubbling and golden.

*Busy mum's lifesaver* Use a supermarket readymade four-cheese sauce instead of béchamel and omit the goat's cheese.

# Baked chickpea and butternut squash rice

This is a kind of vegetarian paella that I make when teenagers descend on the house on a Friday night. It can be thrown together and sit happily in a low oven until required and you can add more ingredients to stretch it, if necessary.

→ Serve with a big green salad.

*Serves 6*
*Prepare 15 minutes*
*Cook 45 minutes*

1 tbsp olive oil
1 large onion, finely chopped
2 red peppers, seeded and chopped
2 cloves garlic, crushed
1 large butternut squash, peeled, seeded and cubed
1 tbsp smoked paprika
400g (14oz) paella or risotto rice
400g can chickpeas, drained
450ml (¾ pint) vegetable or chicken stock (see page 28)

1 Preheat the oven to 180°C/fan oven 160°C/Gas Mark 4. Heat the oil in a large flameproof casserole and add the onion, pepper, garlic and squash. Cook over a medium heat for 8–10 minutes until softened. Add the paprika and cook for a couple of minutes until browned, then stir in the rice to coat it in the oil and cook for 1 minute.

2 Add the chickpeas and stock and bring to the boil. Simmer and stir for 3–4 minutes until soupy. Cook in the oven for 20 minutes until the rice is tender, the liquid absorbed and the top a golden crust. Leave to stand for 5 minutes and fork through before serving.

*Busy mum's lifesaver* For a meaty version add 230g (8oz) sliced mini cooking chorizo and 350g (12oz) cubed pork to the pan before the vegetables and brown well on all sides.

# Lamb, tomato and coconut curry with garlic naan bread

I wanted a meaty curry that wasn't too heavy, so I created this recipe specially for the book – and I've been making it ever since. It's fragrant with spices while the acidity of the tomatoes cuts through the richness of the lamb. It does need a range of spices but none are really unusual and all warrant a place in the everyday store cupboard. This is one occasion where the dish won't taste the same if you use a curry powder, so maybe it is one to make once you have got your spice cupboard up and running.

→ Serve with warm garlic naan bread or basmati rice and steamed green beans.

------------------------------------------------------------

*Serves 6*
*Prepare 15 minutes*
*Cook 1 hour 30 minutes*

2 tbsp sunflower oil
2–3 cloves garlic, sliced
2.5cm (1in) piece fresh root ginger, peeled and chopped
1 green chilli, seeded and chopped
1 tsp ground cumin
2 tsp ground coriander
4 cardamom pods, crushed
450g (1lb) cherry tomatoes, halved
1kg (2¼lb) cubed stewing lamb
400g can coconut milk
juice of 1 lime
chopped fresh coriander
salt and freshly ground black pepper

1 Heat the oil in a large heavy-based sauté pan and add the garlic, ginger, chilli, cumin, coriander and cardamom. Cook over a medium heat for a minute to cook the spices then add the tomatoes and stir gently to coat in the spices. Turn up the heat then add the cubed lamb and brown on all sides. Stir in the coconut milk, season and simmer, covered, for 1 hour until the lamb is tender.

2 Just before serving stir in the lime juice and scatter with chopped coriander.

*Busy mum's lifesaver* To make the garlic naan bread, buy good-quality plain naan. Melt some butter with a couple of cloves of crushed garlic and a teaspoon of ground coriander. Brush the bread on both sides and bake in a hot oven for 4–5 minutes until warm.

# Pork and rosemary meatballs with fresh tomato sauce

These meatballs can be made well in advance and served hot or cold, as a main course or as a tapa – with bread to mop up any juices. As there are very few ingredients you will really notice the difference in the quality of the pork you choose. I buy free range and not too fatty.

→ Serve with pasta or rice – or, for real decadence, oven chips – plus salad.

*Serves 6*
*Prepare 20 minutes*
*Cook 25 minutes*

650g (1½lb) pork mince
2 cloves garlic, finely chopped
1 large free-range egg, beaten
6 anchovy fillets, finely chopped
3 tbsp fresh rosemary leaves, finely
    chopped
3 tbsp extra-virgin olive oil
6 large fresh plum tomatoes,
    coarsely chopped
1 tbsp balsamic vinegar
2 tbsp plain flour
chopped flat-leaf parsley
salt and freshly ground black pepper

1 Mix the mince, garlic, egg, anchovies, rosemary and seasoning together in a mixing bowl until thoroughly combined. The easiest way to do this is with your hands. Roll into small balls – you should make about 24. Cover and chill while you make the sauce.

2 Heat a tablespoon of oil in a medium pan, add the tomatoes and season. Simmer for 5 minutes until pulpy. Stir in the balsamic vinegar and keep warm.

3 Roll the meatballs in the flour. Heat the remaining oil in a non-stick frying pan and fry the meatballs in three batches for 5–6 minutes until browned all over and cooked through. Drain on kitchen paper and add to the tomato sauce. Simmer for a minute or two then serve, scattered with flat-leaf parsley.

*Busy mum's lifesaver* If you can't find ripe plum tomatoes use a can of plum tomatoes or replace the homemade sauce with a readymade chilled tomato sauce for pasta (these are really not too bad in an emergency).

# Soy and honey slow-cooked belly pork

A wonderful dish that can be left in the oven for hours at a low setting – in fact, the longer you cook it the better. Or transfer it to a slow cooker once you've added the spices and brought the dish to the boil. ⟶ Serve with sticky Thai-style rice to sop up the juices and stir-fry some broccoli or spinach to complete the meal.

*Serves 6*
*Prepare 15 minutes*
*Cook 4 hours*

1.5kg (3¼lb) belly pork (with no bones)
150ml (¼ pint) medium sherry or rice wine
150ml (¼ pint) soy sauce
1 tsp Chinese five-spice powder
5cm (2in) piece fresh ginger, peeled and sliced
1 red chilli, deseeded and chopped
2–3 cloves garlic, crushed
2 tbsp thick honey
3 tbsp chopped fresh coriander

1 Preheat the oven to 150°C/fan oven 130°C/Gas Mark 2. Place the pork in a large flameproof casserole, add enough water to almost cover then pour in the sherry and soy sauce. Add the five-spice powder, ginger, chilli, garlic and honey. Bring to the boil on top of the stove then cover the pan and cook in the oven for 3–3½ hours until the pork is really soft and tender.

2 Take the casserole out of the oven. Lift the pork out of the cooking juices. Remove and discard the skin and some of the fat with a sharp knife. It comes off easily. Transfer the pork to a warm serving dish, cover and leave to stand.

3 Return the casserole to the hob and simmer the sauce until reduced by half. Stir in the chopped coriander and serve with the pork, carved into thick slices.

*Busy mum's lifesaver* Cook belly pork slowly to melt and soften the rind and fat. If you don't cook it for long enough it will be fatty and unpleasant – there are no short cuts. The preparation is so simple you could leave it to cook for half a day. It can also be made a day ahead and then reheated, which will intensify the flavour.

# Smoked haddock potato gratin

*Pommes dauphinoise* – sliced potatoes cooked with garlic and cream – layered with smoked haddock. It's a marriage made in heaven; an easy take on a fish pie that makes a great winter supper dish (Rick Stein does something similar with Arbroath smokies).

⟶ Serve with a green salad or peas.

*Serves 6*
*Prepare 15 minutes*
*Cook 1 hour*

1kg (2¼lb) smoked haddock fillets
450ml (¾ pint) semi-skimmed milk
2 fresh bay leaves
1.2kg (2½lb) floury potatoes such as
    Maris Piper, peeled and thinly sliced
2 cloves garlic, crushed
25g (1oz) butter
300ml (½ pint) double cream
salt and freshly ground black pepper

1 Preheat the oven to 200°C/fan oven 180°C/Gas Mark 6. Place the haddock in a pan, add the milk and the bay leaves and bring to the boil. Poach gently for 5–6 minutes until just cooked through – the flesh should just flake easily without falling apart. Drain off the cooking liquid and reserve. Flake the fish, discarding the skin.

2 Layer up the sliced potatoes and flaked fish with the garlic and plenty of seasoning in a well-buttered 1.75 litre (3 pint) shallow ovenproof dish, ending with a neat layer of potatoes. Dot with butter and pour over the reserved cooking milk and cream.

3 Bake in the oven for 50–60 minutes until the potato is tender and the top golden and crisp. Cover with foil if the top gets too brown.

# Italian beef bake

Strictly speaking, this is a version of cottage pie but with added flavourings and a wonderfully stringy mozzarella and potato topping. It's a really good party dish, popular with younger people.
→ Serve with a big green salad.

---

*Serves 6–8*
*Prepare 25 minutes*
*Cook 1 hour 45 minutes*

2 tbsp olive oil
2 medium onions, sliced
2 cloves garlic, crushed
100g (4oz) unsmoked bacon
   cubes (lardons)
1kg (2¼lb) beef mince
400g can Italian plum tomatoes
juice and rind of ½ orange
2 bay leaves
1.35kg (3lb) Maris Piper potatoes,
   peeled
100g (4oz) mozzarella, sliced
150ml (¼ pint) single cream
2 tbsp grated Parmesan
salt and freshly ground black pepper

1 Heat the oil in a large non-stick frying pan and add the onions and garlic. Cook for 3–4 minutes until soft but not browned. Add the bacon and cook for a further 5 minutes, then add the mince and brown well. Add the tomatoes, orange rind and juice, bay leaves and seasoning and bring to the boil. Cover and simmer for 45 minutes until reduced and tomatoey.

2 Meanwhile place the whole potatoes in cold water to cover, then bring to the boil and simmer for 15–20 minutes until just tender. Drain and leave until cool enough to handle. Slice thinly.

3 Preheat the oven to 220°C/fan oven 200°C/Gas Mark 7. Spoon the meat mixture into a shallow 3 litre (5 pint) ovenproof dish. Arrange the potato slices over the meat, interspersing with the sliced mozzarella. Season well. Pour over the cream and scatter with the Parmesan. Bake for 40–45 minutes until the topping is bubbling and golden.

# magic
# meals

When you're struggling to get everyone organised at breakfast time, it's hard to put much effort into packing up a nutritious lunch box. I still tremble when recalling the horror of some school mornings – when a child announced they needed a costume for a play/ingredients for a cookery class/ picking up from a match miles across town. All as I was getting ready to catch an early train while putting the washing on and trying to assemble packed lunches that would actually be eaten – rather than stay at the bottom of the school bag.

These recipes are the solution. They're based around meals cooked the night before that, with a little tweaking, transform into the centrepiece of a packed lunch for children and – in budget-conscious times – for working adults too. ➞

# Easy vegetable samosas

Make up a batch of samosas and freeze some after you've cooked them – then they'll be ready for emergency suppers or snacks. I like to vary the size so that some can be eaten easily without a knife and fork, while larger versions are a bit like a pasty. They're a good way of using up leftover vegetables.

➝ Serve with salad and a mango yogurt dip (see page 120).

*Makes 4–8 depending on size*
*Prepare 15 minutes*
*Cook 30 minutes*

175g (6oz) frozen peas or frozen
    vegetable mix
3 tbsp groundnut oil
1 small onion, thinly sliced
2 cloves garlic, crushed
2 medium cooked potatoes, diced
2–3 tsp medium curry powder
1 tsp cumin seeds
2–3 tbsp chopped fresh mint
8 sheets filo pastry
salt and freshly ground black pepper

1 Preheat the oven to 220°C/fan oven 200°C/Gas Mark 7. Cook the peas in boiling water for a minute or two and drain thoroughly. Heat half the oil in a frying pan and add the onion and garlic. Cook over a medium heat for 5 minutes until softened and starting to brown. Add the potatoes and cook for a further couple of minutes until golden. Stir in the curry powder and cumin and cook for a further minute. Stir in the peas, mint and seasoning.

2 Brush the filo sheets with the remaining oil and layer the sheets in pairs so you have four double sheets of pastry. Cut in half across the diagonal. Place a spoonful of the filling on one end of a double triangle of pastry and fold over to cover the filling, then keep folding until you have a triangular parcel. Pinch the edges together to seal. Place on a dampened baking sheet and bake for 15–20 minutes until crisp and golden.

# Mango glazed sausages

This is a twist on the popular honey and mustard glazed sausages often served at parties. Mango chutney and tomato ketchup give a lovely sweet and sour finish that tastes fantastic cold. Save some cooked potatoes to go with the sausages for a filling lunch box.

➝ Serve the sausages with baked potatoes and green beans.

*Serves 4*
*Prepare 15 minutes*
*Cook 30 minutes*

500g (1lb 2oz) good pork sausages
3 tbsp tomato ketchup
3 tbsp mango chutney
1 tsp chilli sauce (optional)
salt and freshly ground black pepper

1 Preheat the oven to 200°C/fan oven 180°C/Gas Mark 6. Squeeze the sausages in the middle and twist, then cut each one into two small sausages. Place them in a shallow ovenproof dish or roasting tin so they fit snugly in a single layer. Mix together the ketchup, mango chutney, chilli sauce and seasoning and spoon over the sausages.

2 Cook for 25–30 minutes, basting with the sauce occasionally, until golden and gooey.

# Pea and pepper frittata

A versatile Italian omelette cake that's great hot or cold. It's a good recipe for leftover cooked vegetables and bits of cheese that need using up: try it with shredded cooked greens, spinach, diced courgette, broccoli or sweetcorn, or your family's favourite combination.

→ Serve with a tomato salad.

*Serves 4*
*Prepare 15 minutes*
*Cook 15 minutes*

200g (7oz) frozen peas
2 tbsp olive oil
1 small red onion, finely chopped
2 red peppers, seeded and sliced
8 large free-range eggs, beaten
2 tbsp semi-skimmed milk
50g (2oz) feta cheese, diced
salt and freshly ground black pepper

1 Cook the peas in boiling water for a minute or two and drain thoroughly. Heat half the oil in a frying pan and add the onion and pepper. Cook over a medium heat for 5 minutes until softened and starting to brown. Add the peas and mix well. Season.

2 Preheat the grill. Stir the pea mixture into the beaten eggs with the milk, feta and seasoning. Heat the remaining oil in a non-stick frying pan over a medium heat, add the egg mixture and stir to bring the cooked egg to the centre, allowing any runny egg to cook. Continue to cook for 3–4 minutes until the base is browned and the egg is almost set. Place the pan under the grill for 2–3 minutes to brown the top. Serve warm or cold cut into wedges.

*Busy mum's lifesaver* Wrap wedges of frittata in foil for packed lunches.

# My mum's oven-fried chicken with sweetcorn salsa

This recipe uses a readymade stuffing mix and there is no deep-frying involved. Egging and breadcrumbing the chicken is a little bit of a fiddle, though, so for that reason I often make up a double batch and freeze one lot uncooked for later. My mother made this dish for my sisters and me when we were children and it's still a favourite.

⟶ Serve with baked potatoes.

---

*Serves 4*
*Prepare 15 minutes*
*Cook 40 minutes*

2 tbsp plain flour
8 small skinless free-range chicken
   thigh fillets
1 free-range egg, beaten
75g (3oz) good-quality dried sage and
   onion stuffing mix (check the
   ingredients list)
2 tbsp olive oil
200g can sweetcorn, drained
4 salad onions, sliced
1 red pepper, seeded and chopped
2 tbsp Thai sweet chilli sauce
salt and freshly ground black pepper

**1** Preheat the oven to 200°C/fan oven 180°C/Gas Mark 6. Season the flour and dip the chicken thighs into the flour, then into the egg and finally into the stuffing mix – try to coat them completely. Place the thighs in a roasting tin and drizzle with the oil.

**2** Cook in the oven for 30–40 minutes, turning once, until crisp and golden and the chicken is cooked through.

**3** While the chicken is cooking, drain the sweetcorn and mix with the sliced salad onions, chopped pepper and chilli sauce. Serve with the cooked chicken.

*Busy mum's lifesaver* Wrap up any cold leftovers in foil for lunch boxes. Pack the salsa in a separate sealed pot.

# Caramelised onion, goat's cheese and pine-nut tarts

This recipe takes no time at all. It uses one of those ready-rolled sheets of pastry and, if you're in a real hurry, there's always readymade onion marmalade. For an evening meal you could cook the mixture as a large 18–20cm (7–8in) tart, but these little versions are more fun for lunch boxes.

→ Serve with a green salad.

---

*Makes 6*
*Prepare 15 minutes*
*Cook 35 minutes*

1 sheet shortcrust pastry, thawed
    if frozen
1 tbsp olive oil
2 large onions, thinly sliced
1 tbsp chopped fresh thyme
25g (1oz) raisins
25g (1oz) pine nuts
1 tbsp red pesto
50g (2oz) firm goat's cheese, grated
salt and freshly ground black pepper

1 Preheat the oven to 200°C/fan oven 180°C/Gas Mark 6. Cut out 6 x 10cm (4in) rounds from the pastry sheet and press gently into large muffin tins, leaving the edges rough. Reroll any trimmings on a floured surface if needed. Chill the pastry cases in the fridge.

2 For the filling, heat the oil in a frying pan and add the onions. Cook very gently for 10 minutes until softened but not browned, then increase the temperature and cook for 3–4 minutes until golden brown. Stir in the thyme, raisins, pine nuts and seasoning.

3 Spoon a little pesto into the base of the tarts and top with the onion mixture. Scatter with grated goat's cheese. Bake for 15–18 minutes until golden and cooked through. Serve hot or cold.

*Busy mum's lifesaver* The firm texture makes these tarts easy to transport. Wrap them in foil and keep chilled until needed.

# Sticky pork saté with peanut butter dipping sauce

Peanut butter transforms into a delicious dipping sauce that can be stored in the fridge to serve with these easy saté or any grilled meats. Use chicken instead if your children don't like pork.

➜ Serve with mini pittas to mop up any extra sauce.

---

*Serves 3–4*
*Prepare 10 minutes plus 15 minutes*
*    marinating time*
*Cook 15 minutes*

350g (12oz) pork fillet, cut into 5cm (2in) strips
½ tsp dried crushed chillies
juice of 1 lime
2 tbsp light brown muscovado sugar
2 tbsp soy sauce
5 tbsp crunchy peanut butter
1 tsp shrimp paste or anchovy essence (optional)
150ml (¼ pint) coconut milk
shredded cucumber
shredded salad onions

1 Place the pork strips in a shallow dish. Mix together the chillies, half the lime juice, half the sugar and half the soy sauce. Pour over the pork, cover and marinate for 15 minutes.

2 To make the peanut sauce, place the peanut butter in a small pan with 50ml (2floz) water and stir over a low heat until mixed. Off the heat add the remaining lime juice, sugar, soy sauce, shrimp paste and coconut milk, stirring to make a thick sauce. Return to the heat and simmer gently.

3 Preheat the grill. Thread five or six pieces of pork on to wooden skewers. Grill for 6–7 minutes a side and serve on a bed of shredded cucumber and salad onions. Delicious hot or cold.

*Busy mum's lifesaver* Mini saté on cocktail sticks are ideal for packed lunches – or just do cubes of meat if the school frowns on pointed sticks. Pack in an airtight container with the shredded veg and put the dipping sauce in a separate sealed pot.

# Roasted squash and lentil salad

Serve this salad for supper then send them off to school with the leftovers the following day. You can vary the ingredients – another favourite combination is peas, roasted red peppers and pine nuts. Try stirring in cubed feta if you have some spare.

→ Serve with grilled chicken or salmon.

*Serves 4*
*Prepare 15 minutes*
*Cook 25 minutes*

1 medium butternut squash, peeled, seeded and cubed
3 tbsp extra-virgin olive oil
1 clove garlic, crushed
1 tsp cumin seeds
230g (8oz) Puy lentils
2 bay leaves
1 tbsp red wine vinegar
3 tbsp chopped fresh mint
25g (1oz) walnut pieces, roughly chopped
6 salad onions, sliced
salt and freshly ground black pepper

1 Preheat the oven to 220°C/fan oven 200°C/ Gas Mark 7. Place the squash in a roasting tin, scatter with a tablespoon of the oil, plus garlic, cumin and seasoning. Roast for 25 minutes until charred.

2 While the squash is cooking, place the lentils and bay leaves in a pan with enough cold water to cover generously. Bring to the boil and simmer for 15 minutes until just tender. Drain and remove the bay leaves.

3 Place the remaining oil, vinegar and seasoning in a bowl. Add the drained warm lentils, mint, walnuts, salad onions and roasted squash. Toss gently together and serve.

*Busy mum's lifesaver* Pack leftovers in an airtight container and add a small tub of hummus and pitta bread fingers for a filling packed lunch. For real emergencies buy ready-cooked lentils in a sachet – better to be prepared than go hungry.

# Mango and coriander couscous salad

A fresh-tasting salad – its flavour improves overnight. Always use a curry paste rather than powder for making a dressing or adding to a raw dish as the spices will have already been cooked to develop the flavour. Otherwise you end up with a harsh-tasting dish.

→ Serve with grilled chicken brushed with harissa paste (see recipe introduction on page 109).

*Serves 4*
*Prepare 15 minutes*
*Cook 5 minutes*

230g (8oz) couscous
3 tbsp sunflower or groundnut oil
1 small ripe mango
bunch of salad onions, chopped
4 tbsp pumpkin seeds
50g (2oz) roasted cashew nuts
2 tsp medium curry paste
grated rind and juice of 1 lime
4 tbsp chopped fresh coriander (or
    fresh mint)
salt and freshly ground black pepper
lime wedges, to serve

1 Place the couscous in a large bowl and pour on 400ml (14floz) boiling water. Add a tablespoon of the oil. Stir, cover the bowl and leave to stand for 5 minutes. Then stir through to break up the grains.

2 Cut the mango flesh away from the stone and peel. Cut into small cubes and add to the couscous with any juices. Stir in the salad onions, pumpkin seeds and cashew nuts.

3 Whisk together the curry paste, lime rind and juice, coriander, remaining oil and seasoning. Stir into the couscous to coat in the dressing. Spoon into a serving dish and serve with extra lime wedges.

*Busy mum's lifesaver* Pack leftovers into an airtight container, along with some cubed feta or grilled sausage, to be piled into pittas for lunch.

# transient teenagers

Now my family are no longer regularly at home all the time, I find myself wishing they were around more – but the going did get a bit tough in the middle. And one of the main flashpoints was food, often along the lines of – Daughter: 'Why is there never any food in the house?' Me: 'Well, there was plenty last week when you said you had ten friends coming for the night before a party and then you suddenly decided it was not worth going to.' Versions of this conversation do still take place, but not as often. We discovered that the answer was flexibility on both sides: I learnt to keep various ingredients and dishes on permanent standby in the fridge or freezer; they learnt to cook for themselves using the ingredients that I made sure were to hand. Smiles all round!

Whether you've got hungry teenagers who never seem to stop eating (but not necessarily when and what you had planned for them), younger children coming in famished from school or a partner who likes to graze straight from the fridge, these recipes provide the perfect stopgap and mean they won't be filling up on crisps, biscuits and sweets. I've included some easy combinations that will happily sit waiting in the fridge or can be rustled up in minutes – even by teenagers who don't want to cook. ➞

# Baked pumpkin gratin with crusty Parmesan and seed topping

This dish takes little preparation, cooks in one pan in the oven, can be served as a main course or accompaniment, and eaten hot or cold. Perfect! Editing a vegetarian magazine for more than four years gave me the opportunity to discover just how well it is possible to eat without meat. And the huge growth in vegetable varieties available has added even more opportunities to cook great dishes. Pumpkins and squashes are some of my favourite ingredients for their colour, flavour and versatility – and this dish displays all of those. Oh, and it tastes really good too!

→ Serve with a green salad.

----------------------------------------------------------------

*Serves 4*
*Prepare 15 minutes*
*Cook 1 hour*

1.2kg (2lb) pumpkin or butternut
   squash, peeled, seeded and cubed
2 cloves garlic, roughly chopped
1 tbsp chopped fresh thyme
1 tsp cumin seeds
300ml (½ pint) white wine or
   vegetable stock
150ml (¼ pint) single cream
25g (1oz) mixed seeds – pumpkin,
   sunflower and sesame
25g (1oz) fresh breadcrumbs
50g (2oz) grated Parmesan
large pinch cayenne pepper
salt and freshly ground black pepper

1 Preheat the oven to 180°C/fan oven 160°C/Gas Mark 4. Place the cubed pumpkin or squash in a shallow 2 litre (3½ pint) ovenproof dish or roasting tin. Scatter over the garlic, thyme, cumin and seasoning. Pour over the wine or stock and bake for 40–45 minutes until the squash is almost tender.

2 Increase the oven temperature to 200°C/fan oven 180°C/ Gas Mark 6. Pour the cream over the pumpkin. Mix together the seeds, breadcrumbs, Parmesan and cayenne and scatter on top. Return to the oven for 12–15 minutes until the top is bubbling and golden.

*Busy mum's lifesaver* Buy ready-prepared chunks of butternut squash if you are in a hurry – and a pack of fresh breadcrumbs too. For strict vegetarians, substitute vegetarian goat's cheese for the Parmesan.

# Red onion and cumin hummus

Making your own hummus takes minutes, is much nicer than readymade and far cheaper!
Hummus has a permanent place in my fridge – it's an easy healthy lunch or snack. Keep a bag of
prepared vegetable sticks at the ready, plus plenty of pitta bread in the freezer, so that it's as instant
a snack as opening a bag of crisps. The easier you make it to snack healthily, the better all round.
➡ Serve with warm pitta bread and vegetable sticks.

*Serves 4*
*Prepare 10 minutes*

400g can chickpeas, drained
½ tsp ground cumin
1–2 cloves garlic, chopped
juice of 1 lemon
2 tbsp tahini paste
2–3 tbsp extra-virgin olive oil, plus
    extra
1 small red onion, finely chopped
chopped flat-leaf parsley
salt and freshly ground black pepper

1 Place the chickpeas in a food processor or blender with the
cumin, garlic, lemon juice and seasoning and whiz until almost
smooth. Add the tahini and whiz again. Add the olive oil and
blend again quickly to mix. Transfer to a bowl and stir in two-thirds
of the chopped onion.

2 Spoon the hummus into a serving bowl and scatter with the
remaining chopped onion, chopped flat-leaf parsley and a slug of
olive oil. The hummus will keep covered with cling wrap in the
fridge for 2–3 days.

# Spiced chickpea salad with mango yogurt

A quick salad that needs no cooking and improves in flavour as it sits. This is a great snack or lunch for older children. Keep it in a covered bowl in the fridge for people to help themselves.

→ Serve with warm naan bread or pitta as a snack – or with chicken tikka and a green salad for a more substantial meal.

*Serves 3–4*
*Prepare 10 minutes*

1 medium red onion, finely chopped
400g can chickpeas, drained
1 large carrot, diced
¼ tsp cayenne pepper
1 tsp ground cumin
1 tsp garam masala
juice of ½ lemon
2 tbsp chopped fresh mint
2 tbsp mango chutney
4 tbsp natural yogurt
salt and freshly ground black pepper

1 Mix the onion, chickpeas and carrot together in a bowl. Add the spices, lemon juice, mint and seasoning. Spoon into a serving bowl.

2 Mix together the mango chutney and yogurt and drizzle the dressing over the salad.

# Cinnamon sugar eggy bread

The complete comfort food for a snack at any time of day, and even better made with a raisin loaf. Use bread that's a few days old if possible as it will soak up the egg better and have a crisper finished texture. All teenagers should learn how to cook this for themselves.

→ Serve with fruit compote or, for an over-the-top treat, with chocolate hazelnut spread.

--------------------------------------------------------------------------------

*Serves 2*
*Prepare 15 minutes*
*Cook 5 minutes*

**2 large free-range eggs, beaten**
**4 slices raisin bread**
**knob of butter**
**2–3 tbsp golden caster sugar**
**½ tsp ground cinnamon**

1 Put the eggs in a shallow bowl that the bread can fit into. Press the bread slices into the egg mixture, turning to soak up all the egg.

2 Melt the butter in a large non-stick frying pan over a medium heat until foaming. Add the bread and cook for 3–4 minutes, turning once, until golden on both sides.

3 Mix the sugar and cinnamon on a shallow plate and add the cooked bread, turning it to coat both sides. Cut into triangles and eat quickly.

# Jane's poached eggs with Marmite toast

Another quick egg dish that everyone should be able to cook for themselves. It's my sister Jane's creation. The secret to poaching is to add a dash of vinegar to the water to help set the egg white, and to keep the water at a very gentle simmer so the eggs don't break up. If you can't stand Marmite, try a spoonful of sun-dried tomato paste or tapenade instead.

--------------------------------------------------------------------------------

*Per person*
*Prepare 10 minutes*
*Cook 3 minutes*

**2 slices good wholemeal or granary**
    **bread**
**8–10 cherry tomatoes, sliced**
**2 large free-range eggs**
**equal amount of butter and Marmite**
    **to taste, about a teaspoon of each**
**dash of wine vinegar**
**salt and freshly ground black pepper**

1 Have everything ready: the bread in the toaster, the tomatoes sliced and the eggs broken into a small bowl or cup. Mix together the butter and Marmite (I use the blade of a knife). Bring a small pan of water to just simmering point and add the vinegar. Stir the water to create a whirlpool and slide both of the eggs into the centre – the swirling water will bring the whites together. Cook for 3 minutes with the water barely moving.

2 While the eggs are cooking, toast the bread and spread with the Marmite mixture. Place on a plate and arrange the tomatoes on top. Remove the eggs from the water with a slotted spoon, allow any water to drain away, then sit them on top of the tomatoes. Season and serve.

# Chicken and pepper fajitas with salad onion and soured cream dressing

Keep the ingredients for this old favourite on standby. If there's time for a more elaborate offering, I heat up refried beans and add them to the mix. My lot all love making up their own wraps and getting everyone to help brings the preparation time down.

➡ Serve with guacamole, shredded romaine lettuce and grated Cheddar.

---

*Serves 4*
*Prepare 10 minutes*
*Cook 35 minutes*

8 medium skinless chicken
   thigh fillets
1 tsp ground cumin
½ tsp chilli powder
¼ tsp ground cinnamon
2 tsp olive oil
2 red peppers, seeded and sliced
75ml (3floz) soured cream
8 salad onions, sliced
8 flour tortilla wraps
salt and freshly ground pepper

1 Preheat the oven to 200°C/fan oven 180°C/Gas Mark 6. Make slashes across the flesh of the chicken thighs with a sharp knife. Mix together the spices and rub over the chicken. Place in a small roasting tin and drizzle with the olive oil and seasoning. Add the sliced peppers and roast for 30–35 minutes until the chicken juices run clear.

2 While the chicken is cooking, mix together the soured cream, salad onions and seasoning. Heat a ridged grill pan or non-stick frying pan over a medium heat. Add the wraps and cook for a minute on each side until just starting to brown. Cut the cooked chicken into slices and serve with warm wraps, peppers, sour cream dip and any other bits and pieces you have handy, for people to assemble themselves.

*Busy mum's lifesaver* Use a readymade fajita mix to rub into the chicken instead of individual spices.

# Warm chicken, chorizo and rocket salad

This salad is as easy to make for four as for one, and it's so simple anyone can make it – though inevitably they'd rather get someone else to do it for them. My husband Derek makes a wonderful version with avocado, red onion and crispy sautéed potatoes. For my take on it I've added chorizo and peppers. Younger daughter's idea of heaven when back from university is to curl up on the sofa in front of some dreadful reality TV programme with this salad on a tray!

*Serves 4*
*Prepare 10 minutes*
*Cook 20 minutes*

350g (12oz) new potatoes, scrubbed
    and halved
2 tbsp olive oil
200g (7oz) chicken breast fillets, cut
    into pieces
150g (5oz) mini cooking chorizo,
    thickly sliced
4 tbsp dry white wine
2 shallots, thinly sliced
200g (7oz) wild rocket
2 pimiento peppers, sliced
salt and freshly ground black pepper

1 Cook the potatoes in simmering water for 15 minutes until just tender. Drain. Meanwhile, heat the oil in a non-stick frying pan and add the chicken and season. Cook for 4–5 minutes until browned and almost cooked through, then add the chorizo and cook for a further 2–3 minutes until browned and cooked. Add the wine and bring to the boil. Remove the chicken and chorizo from the pan with a slotted spoon and keep warm.

2 Cut the potatoes into chunks if large. Add to the pan juices with the shallot and cook for 5 minutes until crisp and golden. Arrange the rocket in a bowl and add the sliced peppers, cooked chicken and chorizo with juices, and potato. Toss together and serve.

# All-day breakfast medley

This takes all the elements of a traditional British breakfast but cooks them in a roasting tin in the oven. I started doing breakfast this way in my Aga but it works just as well in any oven. As usual, the secret is to use good-quality ingredients for the best results.

→ Serve with ketchup – or Worcestershire sauce for more sophisticated palates.

Serves 2
Prepare 10 minutes
Cook 35 minutes

2 good sausages
2 rashers smoked back bacon, rind
　　removed
2 small tomatoes, halved
4 flat mushrooms
1 thick slice sour-dough bread, cut
　　into fingers
2 tbsp olive oil
2 large free-range eggs
1 tbsp fresh thyme (optional)
salt and freshly ground pepper

1 Preheat the oven to 200°C/fan oven 180°C/Gas Mark 6. Twist the sausages in half and cut them to form two small sausages. Stretch each slice of bacon out with the blade of a knife and cut in half lengthways. Roll the bacon around the sausages and place in a small roasting tin. Cook in the oven for 10 minutes.

2 Tuck the tomatoes, mushrooms and bread fingers around the sausages and bacon and drizzle with the oil. Season and return to the oven for 15 minutes, turning everything except the tomatoes halfway through, until the tomatoes are tender and the sausages cooked through. Make a space for the eggs and break them into the tin. Scatter over the thyme and seasoning. Baste with the pan juices. Return to the oven for 3–5 minutes until the eggs are cooked and serve from the tin, accompanied, in my house at any rate, by large mugs of tea!

# Tumbet

This hearty layered vegetable dish with a flavoursome tomato sauce is perfect for both veggies and meat eaters alike. It comes from Majorca which, despite its long-held reputation for mass-market excess, still has a real feel of Spain and its small restaurants serve lots of great local dishes. I roast the vegetables rather than fry them to keep the fat content down.

→ Serve with crusty bread to mop up the juices and a salad.

*Serves 4*
*Prepare 15 minutes*
*Cook 1 hour 5 minutes*

400g can chopped Italian tomatoes
1 tbsp chopped fresh oregano
2 cloves garlic, chopped
3 tbsp olive oil
2 small aubergines, sliced
2 red peppers, seeded and
    sliced
1 medium onion, sliced
1.2kg (2½lb) waxy potatoes, peeled
    and sliced
salt and freshly ground black pepper

1 Preheat the oven to 200°C/fan oven 180°C/Gas Mark 6. Combine the chopped tomatoes, oregano, garlic and a teaspoon of the oil in a pan; season and simmer over a medium heat for 15 minutes until thickened, stirring occasionally.

2 While the sauce is cooking, toss the aubergine, pepper and onion in the remaining oil and season. Arrange over the base of a roasting tin and cook in the oven for 15 minutes until starting to brown. Layer up the roasted vegetables with the sliced potatoes and tomato sauce in a 2 litre (3½ pint) ovenproof dish, seasoning each layer. Finish with a layer of potatoes topped with tomato sauce.

3 Bake in the preheated oven for 45–50 minutes until the vegetables are tender and the top is golden. Leave to stand for 5 minutes for the flavours to settle before serving.

*Busy mum's lifesaver* Add slices of Spanish Manchego cheese (or Cheddar) to the top of the Tumbet for a richer dish. Tumbet tastes great cold from the fridge – my children attack it with spoons whenever they happen to be passing.

# small but perfect

Although we all know families should eat together whenever possible, when you've got younger children this can be impractical. On the whole, children need to eat earlier than parents, especially after a long school day. The recipes here are aimed at the under tens – but you'll probably find older children will still ask for them, as the dishes become family favourites. They contain tried and tested ingredients that, in my experience, most children seem to enjoy. Though when I have entertained children who claim that all they ever eat is pasta with tomato ketchup, I've usually admitted defeat and served it. Quite a few dishes can be served as single portions, depending on age and appetite; some are finger foods; all are really quick and simple to prepare. ⟶

# Henry's cowboy breakfast

This secret recipe makes baked beans extra special. My husband has made it for my stepson Henry since he was a small boy and I begged him to reveal all. For a special treat at the weekend Henry, now a lot bigger, has this on a tray in front of the television, with the dogs on standby to clear up any spills.

*Serves 1–2*
*Prepare 5 minutes*
*Cook 6 minutes*

1 tsp olive oil
1 small onion or shallot, finely
  chopped
200g can baked beans (low-salt
  variety if possible)
1 tsp soy sauce
25g (1oz) grated strong Cheddar
1 slice toasted wholemeal bread,
  buttered and cut into fingers

**1** Preheat the grill. Heat the oil in a small pan and add the onion. Cook for 3–4 minutes until softened then add the baked beans and soy sauce. Simmer together for a couple of minutes. Transfer the beans to a shallow ovenproof dish (a large ramekin is ideal) and scatter over the grated cheese. Grill until melted and golden. Spoon on to a plate and serve with toast fingers for dipping.

# Cheesy tuna pitta toasties

A really quick alternative to the perennial cheese on toast, this snack is easier to eat and not so doughy. You can use all kinds of fillings – I love it with mashed sardines, avocado and red onion – but here is the basic recipe. Keep everything to hand and you can make up a plateful in an emergency.

*Per person*
*Prepare 5 minutes*
*Cook 5 minutes*

1 wholemeal pitta

1 tsp sun-dried tomato paste (optional)

25g (1oz) grated cheese (I tend to use vintage Cheddar but you can go with whatever is in the fridge)

few thin slices onion (any kind)

50g (2oz) canned tuna, drained and flaked

**1** Preheat the grill. Split the pitta down one long side. Spread the tomato paste on the inside of the pitta if using. Fill with the cheese, sliced onion and flaked tuna and press the edges together to seal.

**2** Grill on either side for 2–3 minutes until the cheese melts and the pitta is toasted. Cut each pitta into thick strips and give each person a sheet of kitchen paper to catch any juices. Watch out for hot cheese with smaller customers – leave pittas to cool down for a bit.

*Busy mum's lifesaver* Serve the toasties with cherry tomatoes and pepper and carrot sticks and follow up with what my children call an 'apple cut up', and you've got a reasonably balanced easy lunch for small children. Quarter and core the apple then cut into thin wedges and serve in a little bowl – so much easier to eat than the whole fruit and seems to go down without them noticing!

# All-in-one mini chicken roast

A roast chicken dinner is top of the list of many people's favourite meals. Here is my version for individual servings: it's meant to be for the younger members of the family but since coming up with this method, everyone wants their own little dishful. I'm sure it's down to the way all the elements work together – each mouthful is a little different with a wonderful mix of savoury flavours and textures.
➡ Serve with mini carrots and broccoli florets.

*Per person*
*Prepare 10 minutes*
*Cook 50 minutes*

3–4 small new potatoes, scrubbed
1 tbsp olive oil
1 tbsp chopped fresh rosemary
1–2 small free-range chicken thighs
1 chipolata sausage
1 rasher pancetta (or streaky bacon)
salt and freshly ground black pepper

1 Heat the oven to 200°C/fan oven 180°C/Gas Mark 6 and place a small roasting tin or ovenproof dish in it to heat. Cut the potatoes into quarters and toss with the olive oil, rosemary and seasoning. Add to the hot tin and return to the oven for 15 minutes until starting to brown.

2 Season the skin of the chicken. Twist the chipolata in the centre and cut into two small sausages. Cut the pancetta in half lengthways and roll up each half. Remove the tin from the oven and turn the potatoes, then add the chicken, sausages and pancetta to the pan. Return to the oven for 30–35 minutes, turning everything once, until the chicken is golden and the juices run clear when pierced with a skewer.

*Busy mum's lifesaver* Mix 25g (1oz) white breadcrumbs with a little chopped onion and chopped fresh sage, bind with a little beaten egg and roll into tiny balls of stuffing. Add to the pan for the last 15 minutes. Gravy for one is a hassle: use a little heated chicken stock to moisten everything.

# Chicken and sweetcorn soup

This is real comfort food – warming and perfect for when small ones are feeling under the weather. Use leftover roast chicken from Sunday lunch and homemade stock if you have any – the better the stock, the better the end product. But it still tastes great made with a cube! My daughters asked me to include it here: it isn't my recipe, it comes from their father's partner, who makes it for them.

*Serves 3–4*
*Prepare 15 minutes*
*Cook 15 minutes*

175g (6oz) cooked chicken breast, shredded or 1 large raw free-range chicken breast, diced finely
2 tsp cornflour
1 tbsp groundnut oil
small bunch salad onions, finely chopped
200g (7oz) frozen sweetcorn
1 litre (1¾ pint) chicken stock
1 tbsp soy sauce
1 free-range egg, beaten
1 tsp sesame oil
salt and freshly ground black pepper

1 Toss the chicken in the cornflour and seasoning to coat. Heat the oil in a large pan and add the salad onions and chicken. Cook over a medium heat for 3–4 minutes until lightly browned, then stir in the sweetcorn.

2 Add the chicken stock and soy sauce and bring to the boil then simmer for 3–8 minutes (if using raw chicken it should be cooked through). Whisk in the beaten egg and simmer for about a minute until cooked (it will set into long shreds). Check seasoning and stir in the sesame oil before serving.

*Busy mum's lifesaver* Try adding shredded ham to the soup as well or swap the sweetcorn for a cucumber cut into thin matchsticks.

# Crispy fish goujons with sweet chilli dipping sauce

Make these alternatives to fish fingers with any firm white fish such as haddock or cod. Look out for responsibly caught fish, which is widely available – one day our children will thank us for making the effort now for their future. Coating the goujons in crumbs can be messy, so I try to make up a large batch when I have a bit of spare time, then freeze them for easy meals on busy days. The homemade sauce is made with mild chillies – no heat – children really love its sweet and sour flavours.

→ Serve with broccoli or peas.

*Serves 4–6*
*Prepare 25 minutes*
*Cook 15 minutes*

2 tbsp plain flour
¼ tsp cayenne pepper (optional)
500g (1lb 2oz) firm white fish fillets,
    such as haddock
1 large free-range egg, beaten
75g (3oz) fresh white breadcrumbs
2 tbsp sunflower oil
2 tbsp white wine vinegar
2 tbsp caster sugar
¼ mild red chilli, seeded and chopped
4 salad onions, sliced
salt and freshly ground black pepper

1 Preheat the oven to 200°C/ fan oven 180°C/Gas Mark 6. Mix the flour, cayenne and seasoning. Cut the fish into thin strips about 5cm (2in) by 1cm (½in). Dip them into the flour, then into the egg and finally into the crumbs to coat completely. Place in a roasting tin and drizzle with the sunflower oil. Cook in the oven for 10–12 minutes, turning once, until crisp and golden and the fish is cooked through. Drain on kitchen paper.

2 While the fish is cooking, mix together the vinegar, sugar and 4 tablespoons cold water in a small pan. Heat gently to dissolve the sugar then bring to the boil. Stir in the chilli and salad onions and pour into a little serving dish. Line small baskets with napkins and pile in the goujons, setting the sauce dish on the side.

*Busy mum's lifesaver* Open freeze the coated uncooked fish on a baking sheet lined with non-stick baking parchment. When frozen, pack into freezer bags. To use cook from frozen for 25–30 minutes at 180°C/fan oven 160°C/Gas Mark 4, turning once until cooked through. Buy a readymade sweet chilli dipping sauce to save time, but it's worth trying this recipe at some point – you'll notice the difference.

# Rough and ready fishcakes

A good fishcake is a thing of joy and makes a useful stepping stone to move wary eaters from fish fingers on to more adventurous fish dishes. I usually make mine with salmon or smoked haddock for their distinctive flavour. Adding mashed peas gives a wonderful colour – plus a familiar and welcome taste to most small palates.

→ Serve with tomato ketchup.

*Serves 4–6*
*Prepare 25 minutes*
*Cook 30 minutes*

**650g (1½lb) old potatoes, peeled and cut into small cubes**
**40g (1½oz) butter**
**500g (1lb 2oz) smoked haddock or salmon fillet**
**230g (8oz) frozen peas**
**juice of ½ lemon**
**2–3 tbsp seasoned flour**
**2 tbsp groundnut oil**
**salt and freshly ground black pepper**

**1** Cook the potatoes in plenty of boiling water for 15–18 minutes until tender. Drain thoroughly, return to the pan and mash with half the butter and seasoning. Transfer to a large mixing bowl and leave to cool. While the potatoes are cooking, place the fish in a shallow pan, cover with cold water, bring to the boil and cook gently for 8–10 minutes until just cooked through – the flesh will be opaque. Drain off the liquid and flake the flesh. Stir gently into the potato.

**2** Cook the peas in boiling water for a minute then drain and run under cold water to cool. Mash or process the peas to give a coarse purée. Stir it into the fish and potato mixture with the lemon juice. Check seasoning. Shape the mixture into 8 patties (or 16 mini ones). Place the flour in a shallow bowl and dip the fishcakes in it to coat lightly. Chill until needed.

**3** Heat the oil with the remaining butter in a shallow non-stick frying pan and fry the fishcakes for 6–8 minutes until golden, turning once. Drain on kitchen paper and serve with tomato ketchup.

*Busy mum's lifesaver* Use up leftover mash and peas by making a batch of these fishcakes to freeze. Open freeze the uncooked cakes on a baking sheet lined with non-stick baking parchment. Once they are solid, pack in freezer bags. Use within three months: defrost them first then cook as above.

# Spicy lamb meatballs with cool mint dip

Every cuisine has its own version of meatballs – always popular with children. This is my Moroccan-inspired recipe, simply mixed with fragrant rather than hot spices.

→ Serve in warmed pitta bread with salad and a spoonful of cool cucumber yogurt.

---

*Serves 4–6*
*Prepare 10 minutes*
*Cook 30 minutes*

500g (1lb 2oz) good-quality lamb
  mince
1 red onion, finely chopped
1 tbsp Ras el Hanout spice mix
grated rind and juice of 1 lemon
1 tbsp sunflower oil
16 cherry tomatoes
2 small red onions, cut into chunks
150g (5oz) natural yogurt
2 tbsp finely chopped fresh mint
10cm (4in) piece cucumber, grated
salt and freshly ground black pepper
pitta bread, to serve
salad, to serve

1 Heat the oven to 200°C/fan oven 180°C/ Gas Mark 6. Mix together the minced lamb, onion, spice mix and lemon rind and season well. Roll into 16 meatballs. Heat the oil in a roasting tin set on the hob, add the meatballs and brown on all sides. Add the cherry tomatoes and red onions to the tin and cook in the oven for 25–30 minutes until cooked through.

2 While the meatballs are cooking, mix the yogurt with the mint, grated cucumber, lemon juice and seasoning. Pile the meatballs into warmed pitta bread, add a handful of salad and top with a spoonful of the yogurt.

*Busy mum's lifesaver* Substitute a mild Indian curry powder for the Ras el Hanout mix.

# 3P pasta

That's peas, pancetta and pesto! I came up with this recipe years ago in desperation, faced with a group of hungry nine year olds and a nearly empty fridge. It was an instant hit. My children have always loved what they call 'pesto pasta' and this takes that simple dish just a little further, adding useful vegetables. Don't add salt as the pancetta and pesto already contain a fair amount.

*Serves 4–6*
*Prepare 5 minutes*
*Cook 15 minutes*

300–350g (10–12oz) penne pasta
75g (3oz) cubed pancetta
100g (4oz) cherry tomatoes, halved
100g (4oz) frozen peas
100g (4oz) readymade basil pesto
25g (1oz) strong Cheddar or
    Parmesan, grated

**1** Bring a large pan of salted water to the boil. Add the pasta and boil for 10–12 minutes or according to pack instructions.

**2** While the pasta is cooking, cook the pancetta in a small frying pan for 3–4 minutes over a medium heat until starting to brown. Add the halved tomatoes and continue cooking for a minute or two over a high heat, until the tomatoes are soft and the pancetta is crisp and golden. Keep warm. Bring a small pan of water to the boil, add the peas and return to the boil, then drain thoroughly.

**3** Drain the pasta well and return to the pan. Stir through the pesto then toss with the cooked pancetta mixture and the peas. Scatter with the grated cheese and serve.

*Busy mum's lifesaver* This is a good way of using up leftover pesto. I would choose traditional basil pesto for preference.

# Cheesy tomatoey puffy potatoes

There are so many different ways of tarting up baked potatoes. This recipe is a good way to use leftover baked potatoes and children love the cheesy soufflé mixture piled in the potato skin. When I was a single working girl, baked potatoes served with fish fingers and baked beans was my standard easy meal, eaten on a tray in front of *Dallas* on a Wednesday night. It's one of the few times you'll catch me eating baked beans – with a baked potato.

➡ Serve with peas.

---

*Serves 4*
*Prepare 15 minutes*
*Cook 1¼ hours*

4 medium baking potatoes, scrubbed
15g (½oz) butter
15g (½oz) plain flour
5 tbsp semi-skimmed milk
1 large free-range egg, separated
50g (2oz) grated strong Cheddar
1 tbsp tomato pesto or ketchup
1 tbsp grated Parmesan
salt and freshly ground black pepper

**1** Heat the oven to 200°C/fan oven 180°C/Gas Mark 6. Prick the potatoes with a fork and rub with a little salt. Bake for an hour until the skins are crisp and the potato flesh is tender. Leave until cool enough to handle.

**2** While the potatoes are cooking, melt the butter in a small pan, add the flour and cook for a minute. Gradually stir in the milk and bring to the boil, stirring continuously until really thick. Beat the egg yolk into the sauce with the cheese, tomato pesto and seasoning.

**3** Cut a slice off the top of each potato and use a teaspoon to scoop out the flesh, leaving behind enough flesh for the potato to hold its shape. Mash the flesh and stir into the cheesy mixture. Whisk the egg white until stiff, then fold into the cheese mixture with a metal spoon. Pile back into the potato shells, sprinkle with Parmesan and bake for 12–15 minutes until well risen and golden.

*Busy mum's lifesaver* Cook the potatoes in the microwave if you're in a hurry – but always finish them in the oven or the skins will be unpleasantly soggy!

# Sausage, pea and potato casserole

This must be the definition of total and complete comfort food. It brings together all childhood favourites in one dish – peas, sausages, potatoes and tomatoes in a lovely saucy combination. This is another of my ex-husband's regular dishes that takes some beating. Poor-quality sausages go mushy when cooked like this, so use a good meaty well-made banger for the best result.

*Serves 4–6*
*Prepare 15 minutes*
*Cook 1 hour*

1 tbsp olive oil
2 cloves garlic, chopped
2 onions, sliced
500g (1lb 2oz) free-range pork
   sausages
200g can chopped Italian tomatoes
350ml (12floz) chicken stock (see
   page 28)
1 tbsp Worcestershire sauce
500g (1lb 2oz) old potatoes, peeled
   and thickly sliced
300g (10oz) frozen peas
salt and freshly ground black pepper

1 Preheat the oven to 200°C/fan oven180°C/ Gas Mark 6. Heat the oil in a flameproof casserole and cook the garlic and onions over a low heat for 5 minutes until softened and lightly browned. Add the sausages then turn up the heat and brown on all sides.

2 Stir in the tomatoes, stock, Worcestershire sauce and seasoning and bring to the boil. Cover and transfer to the oven for 15 minutes, Stir in the sliced potato and return to the oven for 20 minutes until the potatoes are nearly tender.

3 Five minutes before serving, stir the peas into the pan, cover and return to the oven until piping hot and cooked through. Check seasoning and serve.

# Little burgers with sweet onion jam

Homemade burgers can be really dry and unexciting, especially when served in a bun of dodgy quality. This version is made with a mix of pork and beef mince, and if you use good-quality mince they should be juicy but not too fatty. I like to make these mini ones and serve them in small rolls – they are easier to eat and have that miniature appeal that both young and old respond to. A little homemade onion jam adds welcome moisture and texture.

*Serves 4*
*Prepare 15 minutes*
*Cook 30 minutes*

250g (9oz) lean beef mince
250g (9oz) lean pork mince
1 tbsp ground cumin
2 tbsp chopped fresh mint
2 shallots, finely chopped
1 clove garlic, crushed
2 tbsp olive oil
1 large red onion, thinly sliced
1 tbsp dark muscovado sugar
2 tbsp red wine vinegar
8 small good-quality round white rolls
salt and freshly ground black pepper
shredded lettuce, to serve

1 Mix the minced beef and pork with the cumin, mint, chopped shallots, garlic and seasoning, using your hands to combine it really well. Shape into eight flat patties and chill until ready to cook.

2 To make the onion marmalade, heat a tablespoon of the oil in a small frying pan, add the shallots and cook gently for 15 minutes until really softened but not browned. Stir in the sugar and vinegar and continue to cook for 5 minutes until golden and thick.

3 Preheat the grill. Brush the burgers on both sides with the remaining oil then grill for 2–5 minutes a side, depending on the size, until the burgers are browned and cooked through. Toast the rolls. Cut the rolls in half. On each bottom half place a handful of shredded lettuce, a burger and a spoonful of the onion marmalade. Top with the other half of the roll.

*Busy mum's lifesaver* Use Ras el Hanout spice mix as an alternative to the cumin and buy readymade onion marmalade to cut down the preparation.

# home alone

This chapter is here for those times when you have to eat a meal all on your ownsome – when the children are tucked up in bed and your partner is away. I know it's all too easy to pick at leftovers – or sometimes just a giant bag of crisps and a large gin and tonic! There are tougher times, too, when you might be cooking for one. I was suddenly pitchforked into single parenthood when my children were still too small to eat an evening meal with me after work, and eating well and enjoyably on my own became a real challenge. So I decided that once a week – usually on a Friday – I would sit down to a proper meal cooked specially for me, served with a glass or two of wine. It was a survival technique that really worked. Here are some of my favourite dishes for those times you find yourself eating alone: they make good light lunches and suppers and I still cook them all regularly. They are so delicious you'll probably want to share them with friends and family too. ⟶

# Tagliatelle with prawns and rocket pesto

Treat yourself to this gorgeously simple but special dish when everyone else is out. You can buy just a few raw king prawns at the fishmonger or fish counter of the supermarket. Or look out for good-quality frozen ones – buy those that can be cooked straight from frozen. I sometimes make it with scallops instead which is just as wonderful.

⟶ Serve with a cherry tomato and red onion salad.

*Serves 1*
*Prepare 10 minutes*
*Cook 10 minutes*

large handful wild rocket
1 clove garlic, chopped
¼ tsp dried chilli flakes
2 tbsp grated Parmesan
1 tbsp extra-virgin olive oil
75g (3oz) egg tagliatelle
5–6 raw king prawns, peeled
3 tbsp dry white wine
salt and freshly ground black pepper

1 First make the pesto. In a food processor or using a pestle and mortar whiz together the rocket, garlic, chilli and Parmesan with 2 tsp of the oil and seasoning to make a rough paste. Cook the tagliatelle in a large pan of boiling water for 4–5 minutes (or according to pack instructions) until al dente.

2 While the pasta is cooking, heat the remaining oil in a small frying pan, add the prawns, season and cook over a high heat for a couple of minutes. Pour in the wine and simmer for another minute until the prawns are cooked through (they will turn pink and the flesh will be white) and the liquid is reduced by half.

3 Drain the pasta and toss with the prawns, rocket pesto and seasoning.

*Busy mum's lifesaver* Use cooked prawns, but only add them for a minute to heat through with the wine or they will be tough. Buy good-quality egg tagliatelle – the flavour, texture and colour are all better! Try doubling up the pesto and freezing the other half or storing it for a couple of days in a container in the fridge.

# Scrambled eggs with smoked salmon and dill

Another guilty pleasure for lunch or supper. Smoked salmon trimmings are ideal for this – or make a veggie version by substituting sliced cherry vine tomatoes for the salmon.

*Serves 1*
*Prepare 10 minutes*
*Cook 5 minutes*

1 tbsp half-fat crème fraîche
1 tbsp chopped fresh dill
½ tsp horseradish cream
1 English muffin, halved
2 free-range eggs
walnut-sized knob of butter
50g (2oz) smoked salmon trimmings
salt and freshly ground black pepper
fresh watercress, to serve

1 Mix together the crème fraîche, dill, horseradish and seasoning. Toast the muffin on both sides. Keep warm. Beat the eggs with salt and pepper. Melt the butter in a small non-stick pan and add the beaten eggs and seasoning. Stir over a low heat until curds form and continue to stir till soft and creamy and just set.

2 Spoon the crème fraîche mixture on to the toasted muffin, place the smoked salmon on top then the scrambled eggs. Serve with fresh watercress.

# Baked eggs with creamy nutmeg spinach

This old classic is perfect for a quick lunch when I'm working at home or for a tray supper. I've found that keeping my own hens has revived my interest in egg recipes.

→ Serve with crusty bread.

*Serves 1*
*Prepare 10 minutes*
*Cook 15 minutes*

100g (4oz) fresh spinach, washed
15g (½oz) butter
2 tsp plain flour
75ml (3floz) semi-skimmed milk
freshly grated nutmeg
2 free-range eggs
1 tbsp crème fraîche
1 tbsp grated Parmesan
salt and freshly ground black pepper

1 Preheat the oven to 200°C/fan oven 180°C/Gas Mark 6. Cook the spinach in boiling water for a minute, drain and refresh under cold water. Squeeze out all the water with your hands and chop finely. Heat the butter in a small pan, add the flour and cook for a minute. Off the heat, stir in the milk a little at a time. Put the pan back on the hob, bring to the boil and stir until thick and smooth.

2 Stir the chopped spinach into the sauce and add nutmeg and seasoning. Spoon into the base of a large ramekin or small gratin dish. Make shallow wells in the spinach and break an egg into each. Spoon over the crème fraîche and scatter with the Parmesan.

3 Place ramekin or dish in a roasting tin, add enough hot water to reach halfway up the dish and bake in the oven for 10–12 minutes until the eggs are just set.

*Busy mum's lifesaver* **Add cubes of quickly cooked pancetta or chorizo to the spinach for a meaty version.**

# Soy-glazed salmon with griddled salad onions

A fast and easy recipe – ideal for those evenings when you stagger downstairs after the marathon of homework/bath/story/bed. It can easily be doubled for when the other half is in. Or he/she could be cooking it for you both while you are sorting out the children. Cook this on a ridged griddle pan – then you get attractive golden bands across the salmon and onions.

⟶ Serve with new potatoes or plain steamed rice.

--------------------------------------------------------------------

*Serves 1*
*Prepare 5 minutes plus 10 minutes marinating*
*Cook 15 minutes*

150g (5oz) skin-on salmon fillet
1 tbsp soy sauce
2.5cm (1in) piece fresh root ginger, peeled and grated
1 tsp olive oil
6–8 large salad onions

1 Marinate the salmon fillet in the soy sauce, ginger and oil for 10 minutes. Heat a griddle pan until smoking, then add the salmon skin side down and cook for 10–12 minutes, turning once, until the fish is just cooked through. Keep warm.

2 Add the salad onions to the pan and brush with any remaining marinade. Cook for a minute on each side. Arrange on serving plates and sit the salmon on top. Pour any juices from the pan over accompanying rice or potatoes.

*Busy mum's lifesaver* Swap pak choi for the salad onions; cook in the same way – just cut in half lengthways. Oily fish skin (such as salmon or mackerel) is good for you but can be unpleasantly flabby – it crisps up when you cook it this way.

# Honey and mint-dressed mango carpaccio with Parma ham

Perfect for a simple lunch or as a starter for supper with friends. The dressing also works with thinly sliced fresh pineapple or melon and I often have it with natural yogurt for breakfast or to finish a meal (minus the ham!).

*Serves 1*
*Prepare 5 minutes*

½ large ripe mango, stoned
juice of ½ lime
1 tsp clear honey
1 tbsp chopped fresh mint
1 slice Parma ham

1 Peel the mango and cut the flesh into really thin slices on the diagonal with a very sharp knife. Arrange over the base of a serving plate. Mix the lime juice, honey and mint and pour over the mango.

2 Chill for 10–15 minutes then arrange the Parma ham on top.

# Watercress, beetroot and Stilton salad

This is a great winter salad – especially in January when you need a boost of colour and texture after all the rich flavours and overdose of carbs (and everything else) at Christmas. Use organic watercress as it has the right peppery flavour.

→ Serve with bread to mop up the juices – walnut bread is best.

*Serves 1*
*Prepare 10 minutes*

1 small pink grapefruit
2 small cooked beetroot (not the
    vinegary ones)
small bunch watercress
2 tbsp pumpkin seeds or mixed seeds
    and nuts
50g (2oz) Stilton (or any blue cheese),
    crumbled
1 tbsp walnut oil
salt and freshly ground black pepper

1 With a serrated knife carefully peel the grapefruit over a bowl to catch the juice. Reserve the juice. Cut the flesh into slices, discarding the pith and pips. Cut beetroot into wedges.

2 Arrange the watercress on a serving plate. Scatter the grapefruit, beetroot and seed and nut mix on top. Top with the Stilton. Whisk together the walnut oil, reserved grapefruit juice and seasoning and pour over the salad and serve.

*Busy mum's lifesaver* Try adding interesting nut and seed mixes – they're very good for you and are lovely on salads. Although walnut oil is ideal for salad dressings, making bread and scone doughs or for oil-based cakes, it doesn't last all that long in the cupboard, so use extra-virgin olive oil instead if you prefer.

# two's company

Even if it only happens once in a while, it should be a treat for you and your partner to eat together at home. It's a chance to enjoy food the rest of the family might turn their noses up at, or to share a luxury that would be wasted on them. It's also important to sit down and make time to talk – and the recipes in this chapter are designed to help you do just that. They are not too complicated, so you won't waste precious time in the kitchen. If you can, cook the meal together – it can be a way of kickstarting the conversation. (This technique also works with teenagers!) ⟶

# Pepper-coated steak with grilled salsa rossa

Steak is quick and easy to prepare. This simple version is a good choice for the barbecue too – you can roast the pepper and tomato over the coals to give the salsa a wonderful kick. Sirloin steak has the best flavour. I don't often eat red meat but occasionally we treat ourselves to this steak supper.

→ Serve with baked potatoes.

*Serves 2*
*Prepare 15 minutes*
*Cook 10–20 minutes*

1 red pepper, seeded and sliced
2 ripe plum tomatoes, halved
1 tbsp olive oil
1 tsp balsamic vinegar
1 tbsp chopped fresh oregano
½ green chilli, seeded and finely
   chopped
1 tsp mixed pepper blend, coarsely
   ground
2 sirloin steaks, about 175–200g
   (6–7oz) each
salt

1 Prepare the salsa first. Heat a griddle pan or non-stick frying pan until hot then add the pepper and tomato and cook over a high heat on all sides for about 5 minutes until the skin is charred. It's fiddly but you can remove the skin if you want to. Chop the flesh and mix in a small bowl with the oil, vinegar, oregano and chilli. Season to taste.

2 Wipe out the griddle pan and heat until hot. Rub the steaks with ground pepper and add to the pan and cook for 4–6 minutes for rare, 8–10 minutes for medium and 10–12 minutes for well done, turning occasionally. Serve with the salsa.

# Pheasant breasts with caramelised apple and bacon

Pheasant breasts are full of flavour and don't dry out when cooked like this, and are a real treat in autumn. They are now readily available from the supermarket or you can ask a butcher or game dealer to remove the breasts for you from a whole bird.

→ Serve with purple sprouting broccoli or a salad of watercress and walnuts.

*Serves 2*
*Prepare 10 minutes*
*Cook 35 minutes*

15g (½oz) butter
2 large pheasant breasts
25g (1oz) smoked bacon lardons
2–3 shallots, peeled and halved
1 small English apple, quartered, cored and thickly sliced
1 tbsp whisky or brandy
100ml (4floz) good-quality chicken stock (see page 28)
salt and freshly ground black pepper

1 Preheat the oven to 200°C/fan oven 180°C/Gas Mark 6. Heat the butter in a non-stick frying pan over a high heat until foaming. Add the pheasant breasts and brown on all sides. Transfer to a warm plate. Add the bacon, shallots and apple slices to the pan and fry over a medium heat until just browning. Add the whisky and flame it. Spoon the mixture into the base of a small roasting tin and arrange the pheasant breasts on top.

2 Cook in the oven for 25–30 minutes until just tender and the juices run clear. Remove the pheasant, shallots and apples from the pan; cover and set aside to rest. Add the stock to the pan and bring to the boil, scraping up any residue. Season to taste.

3 Serve the pheasant with the apples and shallots and the pan juices spooned over.

*Busy mum's lifesaver* Make this dish with chicken thighs for a family alternative.

# Grilled sole with walnut salsa verde

Quick to prepare and fresh tasting, this salsa verde is the perfect partner for white fish. You could make this salsa verde in a processor but for such a small amount it will be easier and have a better texture if done by hand. If you have enough ingredients, make double or even triple to store in the fridge – spoon it on to baked potatoes, serve with burgers or stir it into pasta as an instant sauce.

→ Serve with new potatoes and steamed cauliflower florets.

---

*Serves 2*
*Prepare 10 minutes*
*Cook 6 minutes*

1 clove garlic
1 tsp capers
25g (1oz) walnut pieces
small handful flat-leaf parsley
grated rind and juice of ½ lemon
2 tbsp good-quality extra-virgin
    olive oil
2 large sole fillets, about 175g
    (6oz) each
salt and freshly ground black pepper

**1** Preheat the grill. Prepare the salsa verde. Finely chop the garlic, capers, walnut pieces and parsley. Mix with the lemon juice and rind, and half the olive oil. Season to taste.

**2** Brush the sole with the remaining oil and grill for 2–3 minutes on each side until the fish flesh is firm to the touch and the edges are golden. Serve with the salsa verde.

*Busy mum's lifesaver* As it's just the two of you, buy the best sole you can. Small Dover sole are perfect for this dish: grill them whole – fish tastes better cooked on the bone. Increase the timing so that they cook through. Run a knife along the backbone – the flesh should come away easily. For a tighter budget choose lemon sole fillets or plaice. Cooking fish with the skin on improves the flavour and holds the fish together when you turn it on the grill – eat it or leave it as you prefer.

# Easy Provençal fish soup

You can now buy really good-quality seafood mixes, either fresh or frozen, from the supermarket, plus excellent fresh fish stock. This means a really fine fish soup is achievable without too much fuss. Now my children all love seafood but when they were small they weren't so keen, so this soup allowed us adults to have a wonderful seafood dinner on our own.

*Serves 2*
*Prepare 5 minutes*
*Cook 10 minutes*

2 tbsp olive oil
1 medium onion, chopped
1 clove garlic, crushed
2 fresh bay leaves
¼ tsp saffron strands
225g can chopped Italian tomatoes
600ml (1 pint) fresh fish stock (you can use a cube if absolutely necessary)
100g (4oz) firm white fish fillet (cod or haddock), skinned and cubed
230g (8oz) uncooked mixed seafood, fresh or frozen
salt and freshly ground black pepper
toasted baguette slices, to serve
rouille, to serve (see Busy mum's lifesaver)
grated Gruyère cheese, to serve

**1** Heat the oil in a medium pan and cook the onion for 5 minutes until softened. Add the garlic, bay leaves and saffron and cook for a minute. Stir in the chopped tomatoes and fish stock.

**2** Bring to the boil and add the cubed fish. Simmer gently for 3 minutes then add the seafood; bring to the boil and simmer for a couple of minutes until heated through. Check seasoning and discard the bay leaves.

**3** Spread the baguette slices with rouille (see below), place them in the bottom of warm soup bowls and sprinkle with Gruyère. Ladle the soup on top.

*Busy mum's lifesaver* Rouille is a mayonnaise flavoured with roasted red pepper and garlic. It's a lot of effort to make just for two, so stir a little red pepper pesto into some mayonnaise instead or buy readymade.

# Scallop and leek risotto

British scallops are in season from November till the middle of May and you need just a few to add their sweet flavour to this luxurious risotto. Use a chef's trick for risotto and prepare ahead: stop once you've added the first ladleful of stock. Then finish cooking just before you're ready to eat.
→ Serve with a salad and a really good bottle of white wine – I would choose a Burgundy.

*Serves 2*
*Prepare 10 minutes*
*Cook 25 minutes*

6 scallops with corals
25g (1oz) butter
2 tbsp brandy
1 tbsp olive oil
1 medium leek, finely sliced
175g (6oz) risotto rice
about 600ml (1 pint) simmering
    chicken (see page 28) or fish stock
2 tbsp finely chopped flat-leaf parsley
a squeeze of lemon juice
salt and freshly ground black pepper

1 Wash the scallops and pat dry with kitchen paper. Remove the corals and cut them and the scallops in half. Heat half the butter in a small frying pan until foaming and cook the scallops and corals very quickly on both sides for a minute or two until lightly browned. Add the brandy and flame with a taper. Let the flames die down then season and set aside.

2 Melt the rest of the butter and oil in a heavy-based pan and add the sliced leek. Cook for a few minutes over a low heat until soft then add the rice. Turn up the heat to medium. Mix to coat the rice in the butter and cook for a further minute or two. Add the hot stock a ladleful at a time; stir the simmering mixture until each amount is absorbed by the rice, keeping the mixture creamy. Carry on adding stock and stirring for 15–20 minutes, until the rice is al dente or just tender.

3 Stir the scallops with their juices, the parsley and lemon juice into the rice. Cook together for a few more minutes until the grains are creamy and soft. Leave to stand for a couple of minutes. Serve on warmed serving plates.

*Busy mum's lifesaver* Make a perfect risotto every time. The secret is to keep it at a steady simmer: too slow and the rice overcooks because you cook it for longer; too fast and the liquid evaporates too quickly, meaning the rice is hard.

# Raspberry and orange soufflé omelette

A soufflé omelette makes a quick and easy dessert for two people since you're likely to have all the ingredients easily to hand. Try varying the flavourings: for example, sliced banana and caramel sauce or chocolate chip and cherry. I hadn't made a soufflé omelette since college but I'm glad I rediscovered the idea – they're great.

*Serves 2*
*Prepare 5 minutes*
*Cook 5 minutes*

3 tbsp good-quality raspberry
   conserve
1 tbsp brandy or kirsch
grated rind and juice of ½ orange
3 large free-range eggs, separated
1 tbsp caster sugar
15g (½oz) butter
flaked almonds and icing sugar,
   to finish

1 Preheat the grill. Place the conserve and brandy in a small pan with the orange juice and heat very gently until melted. Set aside.

2 Whisk the egg yolks with the orange rind and caster sugar until pale and thick. Place the egg whites in a clean bowl and whisk with clean beaters until stiff. Fold lightly into the egg yolk mixture.

3 Melt the butter in a 20cm (8in) frying pan until foaming, then pour in the egg mixture. Cook for a minute or two until the base is golden and the centre puffy and set. Scatter over the flaked almonds and grill the top for a minute until lightly browned. Dust with icing sugar and serve with the sauce.

# Balsamic butterfly chicken with thyme-roasted potatoes

Straightforward enough for a family supper but with enough style to make an impromptu special dinner for two. Simple dishes like this work best when really good ingredients are used, so don't skimp on the chicken and splash out on a more expensive vinegar.

→ Serve with lemon wedges and a tomato and onion salad.

*Serves 2*
*Prepare 10 minutes*
*Cook 30 minutes*

300g (10oz) waxy potatoes, scrubbed and cubed
1 large shallot, thinly sliced
2 tbsp chopped fresh thyme
2 tbsp extra-virgin olive oil
2 skinless chicken breasts
1 tbsp balsamic vinegar
juice of ½ lemon
salt and freshly ground black pepper

1 Preheat the oven to 220°C/fan oven 200°C/Gas Mark 7. Toss the cubed potatoes with the sliced shallot, thyme, 1 tablespoon of the oil and seasoning, and arrange in a single layer in a roasting tin. Cook for 30 minutes, turning once, until crisp and golden.

2 While the potatoes are cooking prepare the chicken. With a sharp knife make a cut down one side but don't cut all the way through. Open out flat and bash with a rolling pin to flatten. Season on both sides. Heat the remaining oil in a non-stick frying pan or ridged griddle pan. Add the chicken and cook for about 4–5 minutes on each side until golden brown and cooked through.

3 Drizzle the vinegar and lemon juice over the chicken. Cook for a minute. Drain the potatoes on kitchen paper and serve.

# really good puds

My theory – and I'm sticking to it! – is that we have all lost sight of the fact that food should be a pleasure. There is so much angst and worry heaped on us about how we feed our families, and the so-called mistakes we all make doing it, that it's all too easy to forget the simple joys of cooking and eating. But it's surely no coincidence that when times are hard we turn to baking and find comfort in the type of puddings our mothers and grandmothers made for us.

I'm not telling you to cook a pud every night of the week – that wouldn't suit waistlines or wallets – but once in a while they are a great way to get children to eat fruit. And I really believe that if you serve a delicious homemade pud it satisfies a sweet tooth – I should know, as I have one – and stops you filling up on processed cakes and biscuits. →

# Blackberry and apple cake

This cake is a stand-by dessert in my home at any time of year – I just add whatever fruit is in season so it becomes apple and blackberry in autumn, raspberry and redcurrant in the summer and mincemeat and cranberry for Christmas. Whichever version I serve, everyone loves it!

→ Serve with pouring cream or vanilla ice cream.

---

*Serves 8*
*Prepare 15 minutes*
*Cook 1¼–1½ hours*

175g (6oz) self-raising flour
1 tsp baking powder
230g (8oz) caster sugar
50g (2oz) ground almonds
150g (5oz) butter, melted
2 large free-range eggs, beaten
1 large cooking apple, peeled, cored and sliced
150g (5oz) blackberries
25g (1oz) flaked almonds

**1** Preheat the oven to 170°C/fan oven 150°C/ Gas Mark 3. Butter a loose-bottomed deep 20cm (8in) cake tin and line the base with baking parchment.

**2** Sift the flour and baking powder into a mixing bowl. Stir in the sugar and ground almonds then beat in the melted butter and beaten eggs to give a soft mixture that drops easily off a wooden spoon. Spoon half the mixture over the base of the cake tin. Arrange the apple slices and blackberries over the cake base then drop the rest of the mixture over in spoonfuls, leaving gaps. Scatter with the flaked almonds.

**3** Bake in the preheated oven for 1¼–1½ hours until well risen and golden, and a skewer inserted into the centre emerges clean and dry. Cool in the tin for 5 minutes then remove from the tin and leave on a wire rack to cool.

# Walnut meringue with roasted cinnamon peaches

Meringues are a perennial favourite and so simple to make if you follow a few rules (see Busy mum's lifesaver, below). Assemble the dessert at least a couple of hours in advance to allow the meringue to soften and the flavours to combine and develop.

*Serves 6–8*
*Prepare 20 minutes*
*Cook 2½ hours*

3 medium free-range egg whites
175g (6oz) golden caster sugar
1 tsp white wine vinegar
100g (4oz) walnut pieces, finely
  chopped
4 ripe peaches, halved and stoned
¼ tsp ground cinnamon
2 tbsp light muscovado sugar
juice of 1 orange
150ml (¼ pint) double cream, lightly
  whipped
icing sugar, for dusting

1 Preheat the oven to 100°C/fan oven 80°C/ Gas Mark ¼. Line two baking sheets with baking parchment and draw a 17cm (7in) circle on each. Whisk the egg whites with an electric mixer in a clean bowl until stiff then whisk in half the sugar until the mixture is stiff and glossy. Whisk in the rest of the sugar and whisk until really stiff. Whisk in the vinegar then fold in the chopped walnuts. Spoon the meringue on to the baking sheets and spread out into the circles. Bake for 1¾–2 hours until pale golden and crisp but still a little soft in the centre. Cool on wire racks.

2 Increase the oven temperature to 180°C/fan oven 160°C/ Gas Mark 4. Place the peaches cut sides up in a shallow dish or roasting tin. Scatter with the cinnamon and muscovado sugar and drizzle with the orange juice. Cook in the oven for 20–25 minutes until the peaches are really soft. Leave to cool.

3 To assemble, spread the whipped cream over the top of one of the meringue circles. Arrange the peaches on top and pour over any juices. Top with the other meringue and dust with icing sugar. Chill until ready to serve.

*Busy mum's lifesaver* For successful meringues use older egg whites at room temperature. Make sure bowl and beaters are spotlessly clean, with no grease. Whisk the whites before adding the sugar until they are stiff enough to form little peaks but not starting to break up. When you have added the sugar whisk until really stiff, so the peaks stand upright when you lift out the beaters.

# Chocolate bread and butter pudding

You can use all kinds of different leftover bread to make a bread and butter pudding. Depending on the time of year, I make mine with everything from hot cross buns to Christmas cake. But I think this version really is one of the very best. We always keep a stock of croissants and pains au chocolat ('chocolate bread' to my children) in the freezer for those emergency breakfasts when a lot more people arrive in the kitchen than you were expecting. They are also useful for this popular pudding. I always have plenty of eggs – the other staples this pud uses are milk, sometimes cream.

➜ Serve with pouring cream.

*Serves 6*
*Prepare 15 minutes, plus 15 minutes*
*    standing*
*Cook 30 minutes*

**6 large or 8 small stale pains au**
**    chocolat**
**300ml (½ pint) single cream**
**150ml (¼ pint) semi-skimmed milk**
**2 large free-range eggs plus 2 extra**
**    yolks**
**100g (4oz) caster sugar**
**½ tsp vanilla extract**

**1** Preheat the oven to 180°C/fan oven 160°C/Gas Mark 4. Cut the pains au chocolat into thick slices and arrange over the base of a buttered 1.75 litre (3 pint) ovenproof dish.

**2** Place the cream and milk together in a pan and heat until just simmering. Whisk the whole eggs, egg yolks, sugar and vanilla extract together in a mixing bowl. Pour in the hot cream and milk, whisking. Pour the custard mixture on to the pains au chocolat and leave to stand for 15 minutes so the bread soaks up the liquid.

**3** Stand the dish in a roasting tin and add enough boiling water to come halfway up the sides of the dish (this stops the custard from overcooking). Bake for 30 minutes until the top is puffy and golden and the custard is set.

*Busy mum's lifesaver* Buy pains au chocolat (or croissants) made with butter for this recipe as it doesn't include any extra butter. If using hot cross buns, use 6 and slice them in half through the middle and sandwich with 50g (2oz) butter. Then cut in half vertically and place in the buttered dish.

# Raspberry and ginger cheesecake

Everyone loves cheesecake and this is one of the best. It's based on an old recipe I used to make back when I was a student. I've updated it by cutting the amount of sugar and adding crushed fruit to the cheese mixture, as well as the topping. Make sure you don't overcook the cheesecake or you'll lose the wonderful creamy texture and end up with a rather stodgy cheesy finish.

➡ Serve with pouring cream.

*Serves 8*
*Prepare 15 minutes*
*Cook 35–40 minutes plus 4–5 hours cooling and chilling*

175g (6oz) digestive biscuits or
   gingernuts, crushed
50g (2oz) unsalted butter, melted
400g (14oz) soft fresh cheese (it used
   to be called cream cheese)
50g (2oz) caster sugar
grated rind of 1 lemon
150ml (¼ pint) double cream
1 tsp grated fresh root ginger
300g (10oz) fresh raspberries
3 tbsp soured cream

1 Preheat the oven to 170°C/fan oven 150°C/Gas Mark 3. Mix the crushed biscuits with the melted butter. Line the base of a 20cm (8in) greased spring-release tin with baking parchment. Press the biscuit mix into the base of the tin.

2 Beat together the soft cheese, sugar, lemon rind, cream and grated ginger. Mash a third of the fruit and quickly fold in to the cheese but don't overmix. Spoon into the tin and level the surface, then bake for 35–40 minutes until only just set. Turn off the oven and leave the cheesecake to cool in the oven for a couple of hours. Chill for at least 2 hours.

3 To serve, remove the cheesecake from the tin and place on a serving plate. Spread the soured cream over the surface and top with the reserved raspberries.

*Busy mum's lifesaver* The top of the cheesecake may crack during cooking but don't worry – it will be covered by the soured cream topping.

# Isobel's Black Forest chocolate chip cobbler

This easy pud is wonderful served hot or cold. There is no fussing around preparing the fruit – you simply use a pack from the freezer and make up a batch of scone mix for the topping.

➡ Serve with clotted cream.

*Serves 4*
*Prepare 10 minutes*
*Cook 45 minutes*

450g pack frozen red fruit mix (we use one called 'Black Forest' that includes cherries and blackberries)
75g (3oz) soft light brown sugar
230g (8oz) self-raising flour
50g (2oz) butter, cubed
2 tbsp caster sugar
50g (2oz) dark chocolate chips
1 medium free-range egg
100ml (4floz) semi-skimmed milk
milk and Demerara sugar, to glaze

1 Preheat the oven to 190°C/fan oven 170°C/ Gas Mark 5. Put the frozen fruit mix in a pan with the sugar and cook gently for 3–4 minutes until the juices start to run. Spoon into a 1.75 litre (3 pint) buttered baking dish.

2 Sift the flour into a bowl and rub in the butter. Stir in the caster sugar and the chocolate chips. Whisk the egg with the milk and stir into the flour. Mix quickly to a soft dough and knead lightly on a floured surface. Roll into 16 balls and arrange over the fruit mix.

3 Brush the balls with milk and scatter with Demerara sugar. Bake for 35–40 minutes until the cobbler is golden and the topping is cooked through.

# Pear, blackberry and almond crumble

Crumbles are a good way to get children to eat fruit – and making one is a great way to get them cooking. My daughter came up with this version when we had lots of blackberries but no apples.

➡ Serve with custard or pouring cream.

*Serves 4*
*Prepare 10 minutes*
*Cook 40–45 minutes*

3 ripe pears, peeled, cored and cut into pieces
300g (10oz) fresh blackberries
100g (4oz) caster sugar
100g (4oz) plain flour
75g (3oz) butter, cubed
50g (2oz) ground almonds
25g (1oz) flaked almonds, to finish

1 Preheat the oven to 190°C/fan oven 170°C/ Gas Mark 5. Arrange the pears and blackberries in a 1.75 litre (3 pint) shallow ovenproof dish. Sprinkle with half the sugar.

2 Sift the flour into a mixing bowl and rub in the butter until the mixture looks like coarse breadcrumbs. Stir in the remaining sugar and ground almonds. Scatter the crumble over the fruit and top with the flaked almonds.

3 Cook in the oven for 40–45 minutes until the top is golden and the fruit tender.

# Apple, banana and orange cinnamon sponge pudding

This layered sponge pud is good for using up any fruit left hanging around in the fruit bowl. It's my homage to my grandmother, who was a wonderful pudding cook and made all the old favourites – rice pudding, jam 'top-hat' sponge and, best of all, treacle suet pudding. Perfect at the end of Sunday lunch.

➡ Serve with custard, ice cream, crème fraîche or pouring cream.

*Serves 6*
*Prepare 5 minutes*
*Cook 50 minutes*

175g (6oz) butter
150g (5oz) soft light brown sugar
50g (2oz) raisins
25g (1oz) walnut pieces, chopped
1 ripe banana, peeled and chopped
1 eating apple, peeled, cored
  and chopped
grated rind and juice of 1 orange
1 large free-range egg, beaten
175g (6oz) self-raising flour
1 tsp ground cinnamon

**1** Preheat the oven to 180°C/fan oven 160°C/ Gas Mark 4. Melt 50g (2oz) butter and mix with 25g (1oz) sugar, the raisins and walnuts. Stir in the banana and apple.

**2** Beat the remaining butter and sugar together until pale and light. Beat in the orange rind and egg. Sift the flour with the cinnamon and fold into the creamed ingredients with the orange juice to give a soft consistency.

**3** Spoon half the fruit mixture into the base of a buttered 1.2 litre (2 pint) ovenproof dish. Top with half the creamed mixture then repeat. Bake for 45–50 minutes until golden and a skewer emerges clean from the centre.

*Busy mum's lifesaver* For a traditional steamed version, cook in a buttered pudding basin covered with greaseproof paper and foil, and tied with string. Steam for 1½–2 hours and turn out on to a warmed plate.

# Banoffi brûlée

Fruit brûlées are so simple to make and a great way of using up leftover fruit. This version is a quickie banoffi made with a biscuit base – any ginger or dark chocolate biscuits will do, but it's best with a biscuit that combines both. I use ginger shortbread coated in dark chocolate.

*Serves 4*
*Prepare 10 minutes*
*Cook 3 minutes*

4 ginger and chocolate biscuits, broken into small pieces

4 small ripe bananas, sliced

4–6 tbsp readymade dulce de leche sauce

300ml (½ pint) double cream, lightly whipped

½ tsp coffee granules mixed with 2 tsp boiling water

4 tbsp light brown muscovado or Demerara sugar

1 Preheat the grill. Divide the biscuits between four individual shallow gratin dishes or ramekins. Arrange the sliced bananas on top and spoon over the dulce de leche sauce.

2 Mix the whipped cream with the coffee and spoon over the bananas. Cover the cream with the sugar and grill for a minute or two until just melted. Serve immediately.

*Busy mum's lifesaver* Try this pudding with fresh raspberries or pineapple instead of banana. Use the sticky toffee sauce from page 186 instead of dulce de leche. Make it and leave it to cool first.

# Honey and bay roasted fruit salad

Fresh bay leaves used in sweet dishes are a real revelation. My bay tree was devastated by a cold winter so until its replacement gets going, fresh bay leaves are a regular on my shopping list. They add a delicate flavour and also look attractive and are a talking point.

➡ Serve with vanilla ice cream or thick natural yogurt.

-----

*Serves 4*
*Prepare 10 minutes*
*Cook 25 minutes*

2 nectarines, stoned and halved
2 plums, stoned and halved
2 figs, halved
175g (6oz) fresh blueberries
8 fresh bay leaves
6–8 cloves
4 tbsp clear honey
25g (1oz) butter

**1** Heat the oven to 220°C/fan oven 200°C/ Gas Mark 7. Arrange the fruit over the base of a shallow ovenproof baking dish in a single layer. Tuck the bay leaves and cloves between the fruit and drizzle over the honey. Dot with the butter.

**2** Roast for 20–25 minutes until the fruit is tender and a sauce has formed in the base of the dish.

*Busy mum's lifesaver* Vary the fruit according to what's in season: try apple and blackberry or peach and raspberry.

# Chocolate raspberry pots

This is my version of a pretty and popular French dessert that we first ate years ago in a restaurant on holiday – little pots of chocolate mousse topped with a mocha cream and fresh raspberries.

-----

*Serves 6*
*Prepare 20 minutes plus 2–3 hours*
  *chilling time*

230g (8oz) dark chocolate (60% cocoa solids), chopped
50g (2oz) butter
100g (4oz) caster sugar
4 large free-range eggs, separated
150ml (¼ pint) whipping cream
1 tbsp icing sugar
1 tsp instant coffee granules mixed with 1 tsp boiling water
230g (8oz) fresh raspberries

**1** Place the chocolate in a bowl with 3 tbsp water and melt on a low setting in the microwave in 30-second bursts or place over a bowl of gently simmering water until just melted. Place the butter and sugar in a mixing bowl and beat together until light and pale. Beat in the egg yolks one at a time then carefully beat in the cooled melted chocolate.

**2** Whisk the egg whites until stiff and fold in quickly and lightly. Spoon into six large ramekins and chill for several hours until set.

**3** To serve, whip the cream until soft peaks form and stir in the icing sugar and coffee. Top the ramekins with the fresh raspberries and serve with the coffee cream.

# Sunken flourless chocolate cake

This is a rather rich and dark grown-up cake that I serve for supper parties but all the children insist it's their favourite too. It's really wonderful as a cake but does even better as a pudding.

→ Serve with a good-quality vanilla ice cream scattered with crushed chocolate coffee beans or a bowl of fresh raspberries.

*Serves 8*
*Prepare 20 minutes*
*Cook 45 minutes*

150g (5oz) really good dark chocolate
   (at least 70% cocoa solids)
150g (5oz) unsalted butter
3 large free-range eggs, separated
150g (5oz) caster sugar
2 tbsp ground almonds
cocoa powder, for dusting

1 Preheat the oven to 180°C/fan oven 160°C/Gas Mark 4. Butter a 20cm (8in) deep round cake tin and line the base with baking parchment.

2 Break up the chocolate and put it in a small pan with the butter. Heat very gently until melted. Put the egg yolks and caster sugar in a large mixing bowl and whisk with an electric mixer until pale and very thick – the beaters should leave a thick trail across the top when lifted up, before the trail sinks back into the main mix. Whisk in the melted chocolate and butter, and then gently fold in the ground almonds.

3 Whisk the egg whites in a clean bowl until stiff enough to form soft peaks. Stir a quarter of the egg whites into the chocolate mixture to loosen it. Fold the chocolate mixture into the remaining whites using a metal spoon. Spoon the mixture into the cake tin and bake in the oven for 40–45 minutes until risen and just set.

4 Cool the cake in the tin for 5 minutes then turn out on to a serving plate. The cake will sink dramatically. Dust with cocoa powder and serve warm or cold.

# Baked peaches with sticky toffee sauce

I make this pud when the peaches or nectarines in the fruit bowl are starting to get a little too ripe. You can cook them on the barbecue very successfully – makes a change from barbecued bananas. ➡ Serve with scoops of vanilla ice cream.

*Serves 4*
*Prepare 15 minutes*
*Cook 25 minutes*

4 large ripe peaches, halved
    and stoned
25g (1oz) butter
1 tbsp clear honey
½ tsp ground cinnamon

*For the toffee sauce*
100g (4oz) light brown sugar
4 tbsp double cream
50g (2oz) butter, cubed
½ tsp vanilla extract

1 Preheat the oven to 200°C/fan oven 180°C/Gas Mark 6. Prepare the sticky toffee sauce first. Place the sugar, cream, butter and vanilla together in a small non-stick pan and heat until melted. Simmer gently, stirring, for 5 minutes until thick and golden. Set aside in a warm place.

2 Place the peaches in a small baking dish or roasting tin. Melt the butter with the honey and cinnamon and pour over the peaches. Cook in the oven for 15–20 minutes until golden and cooked through. Serve with the warmed sauce.

# great bakes

All mums should try to bake for – and with – their children, even if it's only once or twice a year. I always felt guilty that that was about all I managed. But the great thing is my three all remember those occasions as really special, so I must have done something right!

I've always loved baking – bread, cakes, biscuits, you name it – so working for magazines such as *Good Housekeeping* and *Woman and Home* allowed my baking passion full rein. Then I stopped for a few years when it became unfashionable – and people accused me of having designs on their waistlines. But if you deny you and your family good homemade cakes, you simply end up buying inferior readymade versions. Unsurprisingly, they aren't as satisfying, so you end up eating more. A few years ago I returned to baking regularly. In that time I've actually lost weight and I think it's because I eat just one piece of a really good cake or one homemade biscuit a day and savour every mouthful, rather than shovelling down a packetful of something not very enjoyable without barely noticing it.

The real secret is to get to know your oven's idiosyncrasies and adapt cooking times if needed. Use the correct tin size and follow the recipe. Cakes and biscuits are carefully balanced recipes, with all kinds of processes going on; only experiment once you know what you are doing. ⟶

# Breakfast Scotch pancakes with maple syrup

Scotch pancakes – also known as drop scones – are an easy treat in front of the fire in the winter with honey or jam, but also good for a weekend breakfast. They are one of the first things my children learned to cook.

➡ Serve with maple syrup (and bacon – more popular with boys for some reason) or with lemon curd and mascarpone, or chocolate spread and ice cream for a pudding.

---

*Makes 16–18*
*Prepare 10 minutes*
*Cook 15 minutes*

230g (8oz) self-raising flour
1 tsp baking powder
½ tsp ground cinnamon (optional)
pinch of salt
1 tbsp caster sugar
2 large free-range eggs
200ml (7floz) semi-skimmed milk
a knob of butter, for frying
maple syrup, to serve

1 Sift the flour, baking powder, cinnamon and salt into a large mixing bowl. Stir in the sugar. Make a well in the centre and break the eggs into the well. Whisk the eggs gently, gradually drawing in the dry ingredients and adding the milk as you whisk, to make a smooth thick batter.

2 Melt the butter in a griddle or non-stick frying until foaming and drop in four to five spoonfuls of the batter with enough room to spread. Cook over a medium heat for a couple of minutes until little bubbles rise to the surface and pop. Turn carefully with a spatula and cook the other side until golden.

3 Keep warm on a covered plate in a low oven while you cook the rest of the batter. Serve the pancakes drizzled with maple syrup.

*Busy mum's lifesaver* This is a really versatile recipe, as you can make savoury or sweet pancakes in different sizes. Try giant ones for big breakfasts or mini versions for serving at parties, and vary the flavourings.

# Pecan and cinnamon marble slab cake

This cake is delicious fresh when the texture is crumbly but also improves with keeping as the spice flavour develops. The recipe originally came from two cooks I met on the west coast of Scotland and I've adapted it so that it can be baked in a large slab in a standard roasting tin. Then you can store half in an airtight container for five to six days, and freeze half for unexpected guests.

*Makes 24 pieces*
*Prepare 20 minutes*
*Cook 35 minutes*

200g (7oz) butter
150g (5oz) light muscovado sugar
100g (4oz) pecans, roughly chopped
2 tsp ground cinnamon
150g (5oz) golden caster sugar
3 large free-range eggs, beaten
300g (10oz) plain flour
1 tsp baking powder
1 tsp bicarbonate of soda
150ml (¼ pint) soured cream

1 Preheat the oven to 190°C/fan oven 170°C/Gas Mark 5. Butter a 32 x 21.5 x 3cm (13 x 8½ x 1½in) rectangular baking or roasting tin and line the base with baking parchment.

2 Melt half the butter and mix with the muscovado sugar, pecans and cinnamon. Beat the remaining butter with the caster sugar until pale and creamy then beat in the eggs a little at a time. Sift the flour with the baking powder and bicarbonate of soda and fold into the creamed mixture with the soured cream to give a soft consistency. Drop half the mixture in spoonfuls over the base of the tin, then drop half the pecan and cinnamon mixture in spoonfuls over the top. Repeat with the remaining mixtures. Take a skewer or point of a knife and drag through the cake mixture to swirl the two together. Smooth the surface.

3 Bake for 30–35 minutes until well risen, golden and firm to touch. Cool in the tin for 15 minutes then turn on to a wire rack until cold. Cut into squares and store in an airtight container.

*Busy mum's lifesaver* Freeze half of the baked cake, uncut and wrapped tightly. Defrost in a warm kitchen loosely wrapped in foil for several hours, then store in an airtight container.

# Sticky sticky gingerbread

A good ginger cake and fruit cake were vital components of family fishing trips and beach picnics when I was a child. I have reintroduced them to my children to take the place of chocolate bars and bags of crisps that seem to sneak their way too easily into modern picnics and packed lunches. Like many spice cakes this one improves with keeping as the ginger flavour develops and the texture becomes moister. Wrap in greaseproof paper and foil and store for at least two days before cutting.

*Makes one 20cm (8in) cake*
*Prepare 20 minutes*
*Cook 1¼ hours*

100g (4oz) black treacle
100g (4oz) golden syrup
75g (3oz) golden caster sugar
230g (8oz) plain flour
1 tsp bicarbonate of soda
1 tbsp ground ginger
100g (4oz) butter, cubed
1 large free-range egg, beaten
150ml (¼ pint) semi-skimmed milk
75g (3oz) chopped soft apricots

1 Preheat the oven to 170°C/fan oven 150°C/Gas Mark 3. Grease a 20cm (8in) deep round cake tin and line the base with baking parchment. Heat the treacle, syrup and sugar gently together in a small pan, without boiling, until dissolved. Sift the flour with the soda and ginger into a large mixing bowl then rub in the butter until the mixture looks like coarse breadcrumbs. Make a well in the centre and add the cooled treacle mixture, egg and milk. Beat well until thoroughly mixed. Stir in the chopped apricots.

2 Pour the cake mixture into the prepared cake tin and bake for 1–1¼ hours until risen and firm, and a skewer emerges cleanly from the middle of the cake. Cool in the tin for 15 minutes then turn on to a wire rack to cool. Store in an airtight container.

*Busy mum's lifesaver* To bake in a slab instead use a 28 x 18 x 4cm (11 x 7 x 1½in) oblong tin and cook for 50–60 minutes.

# The other Mary's Inverbroom fruit cake

This is my godfather's wife's Christmas cake recipe, but it has a wider role than the merely festive. I often make the cake when there is a build-up of dried fruit in the cupboard that is getting near its sell-by date. Then I wrap it in a double layer of greaseproof and foil, store it away to mature and bring it out to go on holiday or to take to a local event. It can take time to introduce younger children to this kind of cake as they can baulk at 'all the bits', but the bits are good for feeding them fruit and nuts, so persevere with small squares. It worked with mine!

*Makes 24 pieces*
*Prepare 20 minutes*
*Cook 2–2½ hours*

300g (10oz) self-raising flour
2 tsp mixed spice
230g (8oz) butter at room temperature
230g (8oz) dark muscovado sugar
50g (2oz) ground almonds
3 large free-range eggs, beaten
650g (1¼lb) mixed dried fruit
100g (4oz) glacé cherries, halved
50g (2oz) mixed peel
2 tbsp brandy or milk

1 Preheat the oven to 170°C/fan oven 150°C/Gas Mark 3. Grease a 32 x 21.5 x 3cm (13 x 8½ x 1½in) rectangular baking or roasting tin and line the base with baking parchment. Sift together the flour and mixed spice. Beat the butter with the sugar in a large mixing bowl until pale and light then stir in the ground almonds. Beat in the eggs a little at a time, adding a little of the flour if the mixture starts to curdle. Fold in the flour, then stir in the dried fruit, cherries, peel and brandy, and mix.

2 Spoon the cake mixture into the prepared cake tin, spread level and bake for 2–2½ hours until risen and firm, and a skewer emerges cleanly from the middle of the cake. Cover the top loosely with foil if it gets too brown. Cool in the tin for 15 minutes then turn on to a wire rack to cool. Store in an airtight container.

*Busy mum's lifesaver* As well as the classic trio of currants, sultanas and raisins try making the cake with apricots, dates or some of the new dried fruit mixes available, such as berries and cherries.

To make a Christmas cake, bake it in a 23cm (9in) round deep cake tin for 2½–3 hours. Cool in the tin then pierce the top all over with a skewer and pour over a couple of tablespoons of brandy. Wrap in a double layer of baking parchment and foil, and store for a couple of months. Pour over more brandy a couple of times and rewrap.

# Cappuccino walnut muffins

Coffee and walnut cake morphs into these scrummy muffins that can quickly be made up and frozen – then they can be enjoyed individually as needed. Like a mug of coffee, coffee cake can be sweet and unappealing if weak and tasteless, so adjust the flavour according to your own taste. I like my coffee strong so these measurements reflect that.

*Makes 12 muffins (or 24 mini ones)*
*Prepare 15 minutes*
*Cook 20 minutes*

150g (5oz) butter
100g (4oz) light brown muscovado sugar
3 medium free-range eggs, beaten
2–3 tbsp coffee essence or coffee granules mixed with 2 tbsp boiling water
100g (4oz) walnut pieces, chopped
300g (10oz) plain flour
2 tsp baking powder
pinch of salt
150ml (¼ pint) semi-skimmed milk
1 tbsp cider or white wine vinegar
a handful of chocolate-coated coffee beans (I used ones with dark, milk and white choc for the photo), roughly chopped, to decorate

1 Preheat the oven to 180°C/fan oven 160°C/Gas Mark 4. Place muffin cases ready in the muffin tin or lightly butter the tin if you don't have muffin cases. Beat the butter with the sugar until pale and creamy. Beat in the eggs and coffee essence. Stir in the walnuts. Sift the flour with the baking powder and salt and mix together the milk and vinegar. Fold half the flour into the creamed mixture followed by half the milk and then repeat with the remaining flour and milk, to give a soft mix.

2 Spoon the mixture into the prepared cases and scatter with the chopped coffee beans. Bake for 15–20 minutes until a skewer emerges with just a few crumbs attached. Leave the muffins in the tin for 5 minutes then cool on wire racks.

*Busy mum's lifesaver* Order giant muffin cases on the internet. They make the finished muffins rather special – great for packed lunches.

# Healthy-ish carrot and banana cake

Surprisingly, this cake is my secret weapon against putting on weight. Snacking is my downfall, but by treating myself to one piece every afternoon, it helps me drop all other eating between meals. I've shared my secret with all my yoga group mums – here's the chance for you to try it too.

----------------------------------------

*Makes 1 x 20cm (8in) cake*
*Prepare 20 minutes*
*Cook 50 minutes*

300g (10oz) plain flour (you can use wholemeal if feeling particularly noble)
1 tsp bicarbonate of soda
2 tsp baking powder
pinch of salt
175g (6oz) light muscovado sugar
50g (2oz) walnut pieces, chopped
50g (2oz) raisins
1 large carrot, scrubbed and grated
2 large free-range eggs, beaten
2 large ripe bananas, mashed
175ml (6floz) sunflower oil

1 Preheat the oven to 180°C/fan oven 160°C/Gas Mark 4. Grease a 20cm (8in) deep round cake tin and line the base with baking parchment. Sift together the flour, bicarbonate of soda, baking powder and salt into a large mixing bowl. Stir in the sugar, walnuts, raisins and grated carrot. Add the eggs, bananas and oil and beat thoroughly until well mixed.

2 Spoon the cake mixture into the prepared cake tin, spread level and bake for 40–50 minutes until risen and a skewer emerges cleanly from the middle of the cake. Cool in the tin for 15 minutes then turn on to a wire rack to cool. Store in an airtight container.

*Busy mum's lifesaver* Try adding a mix of seeds for extra health benefits. Stir about 50g (2oz) mixed sesame, sunflower and pumpkin seeds in with the walnuts. To ice the cake, beat 50g (2oz) soft fresh cheese with 50g (2oz) butter and 100g (4oz) sifted icing sugar and a few drops vanilla extract and spread over the top. Scatter with extra chopped walnuts.

# Double chocolate pecan brownies

After many years of making brownies, I think this recipe fits all the criteria – intensely chocolaty, gooey and made with nuts. The better the quality of the chocolate, the better the finished brownie. Depending whether I am making these for special occasions, to go with ice cream for a dessert or for a younger audience who may be a little less discriminating, I choose the cocoa solids level in the chocolate accordingly. My daughter's boyfriend says these are the best brownies he has ever eaten.

---

*Makes 24*
*Prepare 15 minutes*
*Cook 30 minutes*

150g (5oz) dark chocolate (minimum 68% cocoa solids), broken into chunks
150g (5oz) butter
230g (8oz) dark muscovado sugar
230g (8oz) golden caster sugar
3 free-range large eggs
1 tsp vanilla extract
230g (8oz) plain flour
¼ tsp salt
100g (4oz) pecan nuts, roughly chopped
100g (4oz) dark chocolate chips (optional)

1 Preheat the oven to 190°C/fan oven 170°C/Gas Mark 5. Grease a 32 x 21.5 x 3cm (13 x 8½ x 1½in) rectangular baking or roasting tin and line the base with baking parchment.

2 Place the chocolate and butter together in a bowl. Melt over a bowl of gently simmering water or do it in the microwave on medium power in bursts of 30 seconds. Stir in the sugars and then beat in the eggs one at a time, followed by the vanilla extract.

3 Sift in the flour and salt and fold into the chocolate mixture with the chopped pecans and chocolate chips if using. Spoon into the prepared tin and spread level. Bake for 25–30 minutes until just set and a skewer pushed into the centre of the tin emerges with a little moist mixture. Cool in the tin completely, then turn out and cut into squares.

# Lemon and lime drizzle cake

This all-in-one cake is a favourite with everyone – especially the cook. Just mix it up, bake and finish while warm with a lemon and lime topping. No messing around with buttercream or icing sugar.

*Makes one 20cm (8 in) round cake*
*Prepare 10 minutes*
*Cook 40 minutes*

230g (8oz) butter, at warm room temperature
230g (8oz) golden caster sugar
4 medium free-range eggs
175g (6oz) self-raising flour
1 tsp baking powder
50g (2oz) ground almonds
grated rind and juice of 1 lemon
grated rind and juice of 2 limes
50g (2oz) granulated sugar

1 Preheat the oven to 180°C/fan oven 160°C/Gas Mark 4. Grease a deep round 20cm (8in) cake tin and line the base with baking parchment. Place the butter, sugar and eggs together in a large mixing bowl. Sift in the flour and baking powder and add the ground almonds, lemon and lime rind. Ideally using a hand-held electric mixer, beat until just thoroughly mixed – but don't overbeat. Spoon into the cake tin and level the surface.

2 Bake for 35–40 minutes until well risen and a metal skewer emerges clean from the centre of the cake. Take the cake out of the oven and sprinkle the top with the granulated sugar and pour over the lemon and lime juice. Leave to cool in the tin.

*Busy mum's lifesaver* Have all the ingredients for the cake at warm room temperature to make it easy to mix quickly. Replace the lemon and lime with the rind and juice of 2 oranges for a change. Or double up the mixture and cook in a slab instead: use tin size 32 x 21.5 x 3cm (13 x 8½ x 1½in) and cook for an extra 15 minutes.

# Liza's chocolate chip oat cookies

I still haven't found a better recipe for US-style cookies than this one. It dates back to when my sister Jane and I were friends with two American sisters, Liza and India, and this was Liza's recipe. We used to bake these in their little kitchen when we were teenagers.

→ Serve with vanilla ice cream for an easy (but always popular!) pud or add to a packed lunch.

*Makes 24*
*Prepare 15 minutes*
*Cook 15 minutes*

100g (4oz) butter
150g (5oz) light brown muscovado
   sugar
1 large free-range egg
1 tsp vanilla extract
150g (5oz) jumbo oats
pinch of salt
75g (3oz) plain flour, sifted
200g (7oz) dark chocolate chips

1 Preheat the oven to 190°C/fan oven 170°C/Gas Mark 5. Beat the butter with the sugar in a large mixing bowl until pale and creamy. Beat in the egg and vanilla extract. Fold in the oats, salt and flour then stir in the chocolate chips.

2 Drop spoonfuls of the mixture on to parchment-lined baking sheets with room for the cookie mixture to spread. Bake in the oven for 12–15 minutes until pale golden. Cool for a minute or two on the sheets then transfer to wire racks to cool completely. Store in an airtight tin.

*Busy mum's lifesaver* Use an ice-cream scoop to get evenly shaped and sized cookies. If you don't have chocolate chips just cut a bar of dark chocolate into small chunks.

# Honey, apricot and cranberry flapjacks

These bars are my answer to mid-afternoon hunger pangs, when it's all too easy to snack on high-fat, high-sugar, processed biscuits. They are full of slow-release energy from oats, seeds and nuts, so make a great snack or special treat (also perfect for packed lunches).

*Makes 16–18 bars*
*Prepare 10 minutes*
*Cook 15 minutes*

150g (5oz) butter
75g (3oz) honey
50g (2oz) light muscovado sugar
200g (7oz) organic jumbo oats
50g (2oz) medium oatmeal
50g (2oz) chopped nuts (almonds, walnuts, pine nuts)
50g (2oz) mixed seeds (sesame, sunflower, pumpkin)
100g (4oz) dried fruit (I use a mix of soft apricots, cranberries and cherries)

1 Preheat the oven to 200°C/fan oven 180°C/Gas Mark 6. Melt the butter, honey and sugar together in a small pan over a low heat but do not allow to boil. Mix all the remaining ingredients in a large bowl and add the honey mixture. Mix thoroughly.

2 Press the mixture into a greased and lined 32 x 21.5 x 3cm (13 x 8½ x 1½in) rectangular baking or roasting tin. Cook for 12–15 minutes until pale golden. Mark into bars and cool in the tin. Cut into bars and store in an airtight container.

*Busy mum's lifesaver* Use any honey you have. Thick honey is easier to spoon out and weigh in conventional scales. Runny honey is easy to weigh if you have adjustable scales – just put your saucepan on the scales then add the honey. Using a combination of oats helps the flapjacks stick together: if you use just jumbo oats, be prepared for them to fall apart and create more crumbs.

# index

# conversion tables

The tables below are approximate and are intended as a guide only

## EUROPEAN/AMERICAN CONVERSIONS

|  | Metric | Imperial | USA |
|---|---|---|---|
| brown sugar | 175g | 6oz | I cup |
| butter | 100g | 4oz | I stick |
| butter | 230g | 8oz | I cup |
| caster and granulated sugar | 25g | Ioz | 2 level tbsp |
| caster and granulated sugar | 230g | 8oz | I cup |
| flour | 150g | 5oz | I cup |
| dried fruit | 200g | 7oz | I cup |
| rice | 200g | 7oz | I cup |
| grated Parmesan | 100g | 4oz | I cup |
| fresh breadcrumbs | 50g | 2oz | I cup |

## LIQUIDS

| Metric | Imperial UK | USA |
|---|---|---|
| 5ml | I tsp | I tsp |
| 15ml | I tbsp | ½ fl oz |
| 50ml | 4 tbsp | ¼ cup |
| 150ml | ¼ pint | ½ cup plus 2 tbsp |
| 300ml | ½ pint | I ¼ cups |
| 600ml | I pint | 2 ½ cups |
| 1.2 litres | 2 pints | 5 cups |

*(NB UK and US pints are not equivalent. I UK pint = 20floz; I US pint = 16floz)*

## OVEN TEMPERATURES

| USA | °C | fan°C | °F | Gas Mark |
|---|---|---|---|---|
| Very cool | 100 | 80 | 225 | ¼ |
| Slow | 150 | 130 | 275 | 2 |
| Moderate | 170 | 150 | 325 | 3 |
| Moderate | 180 | 160 | 350 | 4 |
| Moderately hot | 190 | 170 | 375 | 5 |
| Fairly hot | 200 | 180 | 400 | 6 |
| Hot | 220 | 200 | 425 | 7 |
| Very hot | 230 | 210 | 445 | 8 |

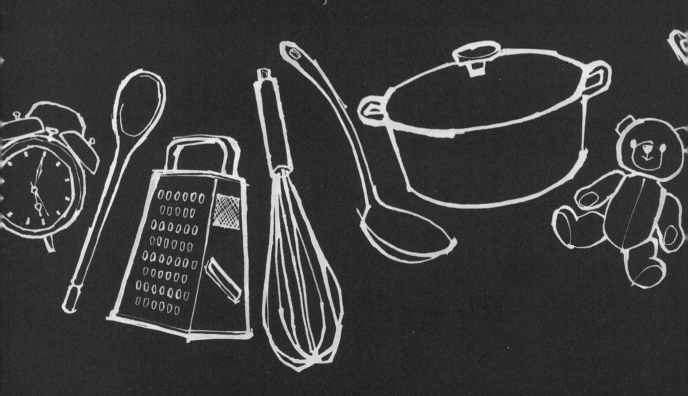